BIBLE SHARING

BIBLE SHARING

How to Grow in the Mystery of Christ

by
John Burke, O.P.

ALBA · HOUSE   NEW · YORK

SOCIETY OF ST. PAUL, 2187 VICTORY BLVD., STATEN ISLAND, NEW YORK 10314

Library of Congress Cataloging in Publication Data

Burke, John, 1928-
    Bible Sharing.

    Bibliography: p.
    1. Bible—Criticism, interpretation, etc.
2. Christian life—Catholic authors. I. Title.
BS511.2.B87   220'.07   79-15006
ISBN: 0-8189-0386-4

Excerpts from *The Jerusalem Bible*, copyright © by Darton, Longman & Todd, Ltd. and Doubleday & Company, Inc. Used by permission of the publisher.

Nihil Obstat:
Thomas M. O'Hagan, S.L.L.
Censor Deputatus

Imprimatur:
Joseph T. O'Keefe, Vicar General
Archdiocese of New York
May 29, 1979

The Nihil Obstat and Imprimatur are
a declaration that a book or pamphlet is considered
to be free from doctrinal or moral error. It is not implied
that those who have granted the Nihil Obstat and
Imprimatur agree with the contents,
opinions or statements expressed.

Designed, printed and bound in the United States of
America by the Fathers and Brothers of the
Society of St. Paul, 2187 Victory Boulevard,
Staten Island, New York, 10314, as part of their
communications apostolate.

1 2 3 4 5 6 7 8 9 (Current Printing: first digit).

DEDICATION

To Margaret Mealey and the National Council of Catholic Women, of which she was Executive Secretary for so many fruitful years.

PREFACE

There is no question that today the Holy Spirit is moving Christ's Church to rediscover the riches of Sacred Scripture. He is creating in the hearts of believers a profound hunger for the Word of God which has resulted in an active curiosity about the Bible: its content, origins and meaning for today.

One of the great fruits of this reviving interest in things scriptural is the phenomenal rise of Bible sharing. Bible sharing is ultimately a simple but life-transforming Christian activity. Groups of Christians are meeting on a regular basis to talk about the Bible and what it means to them. They come together frequently to discuss Scripture and to pray, often without benefit of priest or teacher.

I have found vibrant Bible sharing groups in large cities and very small towns, made up of the well-educated and the barely literate, cradle Christians and the newly reborn. Some ideas I have heard expressed in the sharing sessions were truly profound; others, "milk and not solid food." Nevertheless all who shared their ideas and faith experiences were sincerely searching the Scriptures for the meaning of the mystery of Christ in our times.

This book is offered as a very practical attempt to make the challenging task of Bible sharing easier and more rewarding by providing certain basic perspectives as well as proven methods for arriving at the total meaning of Scripture.

In times past there may have been a problem for Catholics about reading the Sacred Scriptures "on their own." Perhaps once there was a danger of "private interpretation," but that danger no longer exists when we make use of the rich resources of today's Church. As a result of the personal intervention and encouragement of Pope Pius XII, the fruits of the finest biblical scholarship the world has ever known are easily and cheaply available to us. The magisterial guidance of the Church makes it possible for the most ordinary of us to study and share the Sacred Scriptures with absolute confidence that we shall not be led astray. On the contrary, studying and sharing under the guidance of the Church, we shall be nourished and enlightened. Paul VI says:

> *Through the spiritual dynamos and prophetic force of the Bible, the Holy Spirit spreads his light and warmth over all people, in whatever historical or sociological situation they find themselves* (Letter of September 18, 1970).

Bible sharing helps both individual believers and groups of Christians to grow in the mystery of Christ through a fuller understanding of the Word of God. As a result, they enter into more intimate union with Jesus Christ as their personal Lord and Savior which gives them individually and as a community the power in the Spirit to bear witness to Jesus and to bring unbelievers into union with him. Renewed emphasis on the Word, therefore, necessarily underlies the current thrust of the Church to evangelize.

There is another reason, though, why Bible sharing is so important for Christians today. Sharing the Scriptures is, of its nature, an ecumenical activity. Through no fault of our own, we live today in a tragically divided Christianity which is impeding the fruitful proclamation of the one Gospel message. Pope Paul VI asks:

> *Is this not perhaps one of the great sicknesses of evangelization today? . . . If (we are rent) by doctrinal disputes, ideological polarizations or mutual condemnations among Christians, . . . how can those to whom we address our preaching fail to be disturbed, disoriented or even scandalized?* (Evangelization in the Modern World No. 77).

Bible sharing cannot help but bring us further down the road to unity because the Bible is the common heritage of all of us Christians, whatever our denomination. Studying and sharing the Bible together in the Holy Spirit is a God given way for Christians to learn the truth and live by love. And "if we live by the truth and in love, we shall grow in all ways into Christ" (Ep 4:15).

Contemplation of the Word of God, celebration of the Christian mysteries, many rewarding evangelical experiences and the learned counsel of my Associates at the Word of God Institute have brought this present volume into existence. I am particularly grateful to William H. Graham, the Associate Director of the Word of God Institute, Fathers Thomas M. Kalita, James M. Reese, O.S.F.S., and Alan Smith, O.P., and Jack Wright for their valuable contributions to the preparation of this book.

My thanks also to Kay Panza and her daughter, Mary, and Lee Meyer for the careful preparation of the manuscript.

I pray that those who read this book will be encouraged to begin at once or to continue to grow in the important ministry of Gospel Sharing.

> *Out of His infinite glory, may He give you the power through his Spirit for your hidden self to grow strong, so that Christ may live in your hearts through faith, and then, planted in love and built on love, you will with all the saints have the strength to grasp the breadth and the length, the height and the depth; until, knowing the love of Christ, which is beyond all knowledge, you are filled with the utter fullness of God.*
>
> *Glory to Him whose power, working in us can do infinitely more than we can ask or imagine; glory be to Him from generation to generation in the Church and in Christ Jesus for ever and ever. Amen. (Ep 3:16-21)*

TABLE OF CONTENTS

CHAPTER ONE

THE NEED TO GROW IN JESUS

Many well-intentioned and sincere Christians find that the practice of their religion becomes routine with the passage of time. The excitement of thanksgiving for their new sense of freedom dies down; the perception of their own personal worth as a child of God no longer startles. Stirring acts of praise because of a striking appreciation of the goodness of the Heavenly Father degenerate into mere habit. Religious practices that formerly brought such peace to their hearts are endured out of sense of duty and obligation. The joy that conversion to Jesus brought is replaced with boredom, constraint and discouragement. Bright hope in a salvation that will bring wisdom, holiness and happiness, with the complex demands of adulthood, becomes simply another point of view whose meaning is clouded by unvoiced fears and nagging doubts. Before long evil passions and selfish inclinations reassert themselves with renewed violence. Generous impulses of self-giving are stifled by the growing need for present security and immediate satisfaction.

Paul in his *Second Letter to Timothy* describes this experience as one of the dangers of the last days: "They will keep up the outward appearance of religion but will have rejected the inner power of it" (2 Tim 3:5).

The misery of this kind of routine existence is particularly acute for those who were raised from their earliest years as Christians and who have, therefore, never really experienced an initial conversion and the excitement of rebirth. There is always a danger for cradle-Christians that religion is routine from the beginning, with its values imposed from without; a way of life is followed without really being understood. Imposed values can become unbearably oppressive. Religion—instead of being a source of personal fulfillment and integration—becomes a burden, and frequently a heavy one.

I can remember as a young boy having to endure monthly confession. I stood in the long lines in the dark church going over and over my sins—sometimes even making them up in case I had overlooked any—waiting the inevitable moment when I would have to bare my frightened heart to an unseen voice. I envied my non-Catholic friends who seemed no better or worse than myself and yet never had to go through such tortures of self-revelation. God was in the picture; I just was never sure where. Relief followed my revelation, but its effect lasted only until the next sin, when the "psyching up" for confession began again with many cries for help. "Come, Lord Jesus!" Only now, years later, can I recall this experience of my childhood with sufficient calm to be able to write about it.

Growing in Jesus

The question that begs for an answer for so many adults: How can the believing Christian capture for the first time, recapture once lost, or continue to hold in his heart that precious sense of exciting freedom which comes from faith? The answer is—no matter what the age of the believer—always to grow in the Lord Jesus because in Jesus we come to perfect wisdom and spiritual understanding so that we are able to reach the fullest knowledge of God's will for our personal happiness. (cf. Col 1:9-14)

However, we cannot experience the fullness of joy and peace that comes from union with Jesus through faith unless we know Jesus as our personal Saviour. My own experience convinces me that just knowing Jesus as an abstract but revered hero does not achieve union with him. Grasping the central point of his teaching as a philosophical ideal does not calm the fears of my anxious heart. Eternal laws do not strengthen my weak will. "What should be" usually has little to do with "What actually is" in everyday living.

For example, all of us who profess to be Christian will readily agree "Jesus is the Son of God." I learned that statement from the earliest study of my faith; in fact I have always taken it for granted. Certainly, it is an eternally true proposition. Nevertheless, to assent to it does not do much to ease the burden of the human heart choked by fear, riches and pleasure unless truth has a more specific reality. To put it less reverently: Jesus is the Son of God. So what?

In order to grow in Jesus as a source of joy and peace, we need to grow in our knowledge of him as a living, human being who died of love and was then raised in power. Today, when we are possessed by his Holy Spirit, we Christians share that same power in our own lives—the power of Jesus' resurrection which is communicated to us through the word of God. St. Peter writes:

> *Your new birth was not from any mortal seed but from the everlasting word of the living and eternal God . . . What is the word? It is the Good News that has been brought to you* (1P 1:23-25).

Because growth in the word of God increases the experience of the power of Jesus as personal Lord and Savior, the writer of the *Letter to the Ephesians* prays:

> *May the God of our Lord Jesus Christ, the Father of glory, give you a spirit of wisdom and perception of what is revealed, to bring you to a full knowledge of him. May he enlighten the eyes of your mind so that you can see what hope his call holds for you, what rich glories he has promised the saints will inherit and how infinitely great is the power that he has exercised for us believers* (Ep 1:17-19).

4

The Problem of Growth

Growth in the word of God is a tremendous problem today, particularly for Roman Catholics. As a result, even though they may receive Holy Commmunion each Sunday, the majority of Catholics merely hang onto their faith instead of growing in it. This might seem at first glance, like a harsh statement. Yet, it is not meant to be harsh and implies no moral judgment. It is simply a statement of a fact. Exploring the seriousness of the problem is a good start towards solving it and helping all Christians to grow in their experience of the Lordship of Jesus.

There are approximately 48 million Roman Catholics in the United States today, almost one-quarter of the total American population. Of this vast number, only 3 percent are engaged in any serious study and planned program for growth in their religious instruction. Statistical analysis of the Catholic publishing industry, comparing the sale of Catholic religious works with the total Catholic population, reveals that 97 percent never read serious theological books, significant religious magazines, or even the local diocesan newspapers. Furthermore, the vast majority of Catholics do not read the Holy Bible on any regular and sustained basis.

For some Catholics, formal education in religion is brief and is completed in the early years; they study just enough to receive First Holy Communion and then never study their faith again. Others continue as long as Confirmation before dropping out in their teens, while some fewer complete Catholic high school, college or university. At whatever age their formal education in religion stops, however, personal growth in understanding and appreciation of the truths of the Christian message also stops. The result of this widespread custom is that the majority of Catholics in the United States are trying to live an adult life in a modern, technological, complicated, materialistic, consumeristic and utterly pagan world with the religious mind of a child.

No Hunger for More

The failure to engender an enthusiasm and love for more knowledge of our religion is a singular indictment of the religious education programs of the Catholic Church in the United States today. Even such abstract or seemingly dry subjects as philosophy or economics can be made exciting, and an enthusiastic teacher can awaken in his students a hunger for more that will last throughout a lifetime. Even if the student never goes into the field professionally, he will always have an enjoyable and enriching hobby as he continues to pursue the study of the subject. Yet in the vast majority of cases, this hunger is not generated for the Catholic's most important subject—the study of God's word.

Consequently, having the minds of chilren, Catholics find it necessary to run to their priests for answers to all their questions about religion; and the answers they seek have to be brief, uncomplicated and radiantly clear with no shades of grey, just simple terms of black and white, yes or no, right or wrong, true or false. This can be a difficult feat if, for example, the questioner is a young mother who has just lost her first-born son to cancer and wants to know how God could permit such a terrible thing.

Having the minds of children, uninstructed Catholics have the reactions of children. When the answer is not quick, and in accord with their wishes or expectations, the questioners become unsettled, insecure, confused and, as I have seen so often, embittered. Then, they stop asking questions of priests. Because they have no habit of thought which leads them to search out the answers for themselves from the pages of Sacred Scripture or the documents of the Church, they hover in a limbo of doubt and distrust.

I remember one incident very vividly. I was preaching a parish renewal when, during our evening discussion, a man asked me a not unusual question. He was in his fifties, a distinguished and highly educated judge in the town, a Catholic from the cradle and a pillar of the church, who served both as a lector and as president of the parish council. His question was direct: "When are all these changes in liturgy going to end? Every time I go to Mass it is something new. When is it going to stop?"

I replied: "Well, sir, that is easy to answer. There is a little book out; in fact, it isn't even a book, but a pamphlet. It would probably take you no more than an hour to read, but if you did you would have all the answers to your questions about the liturgy because it contains all the principles that govern what is happening in the liturgy—all the principles for change, renewal and reform. It is called *The Constitution on the Sacred Liturgy*; it was issued by the Second Vatican Council, and it is the road map for the future of the Church's liturgical life."

He responded to me with great irritation and actual disdain, "I haven't the time to read all that stuff. I'm a busy man."

That intelligent, mature man would rather spend his days—and evidently parish council meetings—fussing and fuming over the changes in liturgy, ranting on and on in absolute ignorance, than take an hour out of his busy life to personally come to grips as an adult with the principles that govern what should be one of his most important experiences—that of praising God and worshipping Him through His Son, Jesus Christ, in the liturgy. Although he is a mature man and a learned judge, his religious knowledge and attitudes are childish.

Fewer Priests

The increasing shortage of priests is going to make it more and more difficult for Catholics to get the kind of personal counseling in matters of faith to which they have become accustomed. For example, unless there is a dramatic reversal of the current trend through new vocations, in the next ten years one diocese will, to my knowledge, lose 45 percent of its currently active priests through retirement alone! In fact, the shortage of priests is already a serious problem today in many places, with rural missions being abandoned and parishes combined. Where a parish used to be served by two or three priests, sometimes only one is now assigned to meet its needs, although the total number of parishioners may actually have increased. Because of the few vocations each year, both to the priesthood and the religious life (male and female), it will not be long before there will not be enough "professional" Catholics to go around. We already see the consequences of this shortage in the parochial school system.

Consequently, there is an urgency now for individual Catholics to take the initiative in providing for their own growth in faith, to search out their own answers to the dilemmas of life, and to arrive at their own solutions to their problems by drawing upon their own understanding of the rich teaching of Christ's Church. The starting point for such personal growth in faith is the Holy Bible, and so the *Dogmatic Constitution on Divine Revelation* of the Second Vatican Council says: "Easy access to Sacred Scripture should be provided for all the Christian faithful" (#22). Further (#25) it says "earnestly and specifically urges all the Christian faithful. . . to learn by frequent reading of the Divine Scriptures the 'excelling knowledge of Jesus Christ' " (Ph 3:8).

These are strong words and strong exhortations to growth in the Lord. But these words are simply to encourage us to carry out personally the whole purpose of Christian education. The Second Vatican Council, in the *Decree on the Ministry and Life of Priests*, gave priests clear directions about what they are to do as educators:

> *As educators in the faith, priests must see to it, either by themselves or through others, that the faithful are led individually in the Holy Spirit to a development of their own vocation as required by the Gospel, to a sincere and active charity, and to that freedom with which Christ had made us free. Ceremonies however beautiful, or associations however flourishing, will be of little value if they are not directed toward educating men in the attainment of Christian maturity* (#6)

In fact, the Vatican Council actually cautions the laity about putting too much trust in the answers of pastors when it says:

> *Let the layman not imagine that his pastors are always such experts that to every problem which arises, however complicated, they can readily give him a concrete solution, or even that such is their mission. Rather, enlightened by Christian wisdom and giving close attention to the teaching authority of the Church, let the layman take on his own distinctive role* (Church in the Modern World #43).

All of these teachings of the Church lead us to consider the basic questions which this book seeks to answer: How can the individual Christian grow in the Lord? How can he nourish his experience of joy and peace that comes from faith? How can he mature in wisdom and grace?

Plan of the Book

We will begin to answer these vital questions by exploring in Chapter Two how reading the Scriptures, God's word, leads to growth in Jesus as Lord and Saviour. Since Bible sharing is a delightful and fruitful way to grow in the knowledge of Divine Wisdom, we will describe what Bible sharing is in Chapter Three.

To assist the process of sharing, in Chapter Four we will explain some of the distinctive characteristics of the Bible as the word of God, and in Chapter Five we will give special attention to the literary forms used by the sacred writers to communicate divine revelation.

In Chapter Six we will turn our attention to certain theological questions which, left unanswered, can make Bible reading difficult and confusing, impeding personal growth in scriptural wisdom. Chapter Seven will outline two stages in arriving at the total meaning of the Bible for today.

Having dealt with the general perspectives for approaching the Bible, we will give practical directions for forming and conducting Bible sharing groups: Chapter Eight will present the keys to forming successful sharing groups, and Chapter Nine, the guidelines for conducting stimulating meetings. Some forms of Bible sharing that can be used as models for groups are discussed in Chapter Ten.

Because we cannot share our insights into the meaning of divine revelation without diligent private study of the scriptures, in Chapter Eleven we will give a bibliography of some of the best study resources available today.

Finally, Chapter Twelve concludes our presentation by describing how the reader can actually foster the formation of Bible sharing groups through regional celebrations of Word of God Days. It is a fitting ministry for those who grow in the Lord Jesus.

Let us Pray

Heavenly Father, Your Sacred Scriptures reveal the Good News that You love us. You have chosen us to reflect that love more abundantly by professing Jesus Christ as Lord and Saviour. May the Holy Spirit so transform our lives that we unceasingly proclaim the Good News to all creation. We ask You this in Jesus' Name. Amen.

CHAPTER TWO

GROWING IN JESUS THROUGH THE WORD OF GOD

Scripture often refers to "mystery" and "mysteries." Ultimately the Bible is the revelation of the "mystery of Christ" (Rm 16:25-27), and Paul rejoices in the fact that he has been given the special grace of "explaining how the mystery is to be dispensed" (Ep 3:9). One reason for Christians, not growing in the knowledge of their religion today is that they do not appreciate the far-reaching implications of the concept of divine mystery. Not realizing what the mystery of Christ is, they are not motivated to take their growth in that mystery more seriously by making it a true priority in their lives, devoting, for example, adequate time to learning more about it.

A mystery is a sacred secret: it is something which is hidden in the mind and heart of God but which is, to some extent, imparted to us. Since the mystery is in God, it participates in God's holiness; since it is revealed to us, it makes us partakers of God's holiness.

Unlike a human secret, God's secret is not just knowledge; it is power and even glory. The effect of the revelation of this wisdom-power, knowledge-strength is to change those with whom the mystery is shared—changed to such an extent that we can be called a New Creation. Of course, because the mystery is divine, we humans can never fully grasp its fullness. As a result, when confronted with the mysteries of God, we always stand in awe and amazement, delighting in their inexhaustible riches (Cf. Rm 11:33-36).

The high point of biblical revelation is the mystery of Christ because it is the Lord Jesus himself who in his own person encompasses all that the term divine mystery embraces. Jesus is the eternal wisdom of God—the Word—who was made flesh so that we might know him, love him, and be united to him forever. Jesus is God and man: living, teaching, healing and submitting—even to death on a cross. Jesus in his own person brings us knowledge of God and enables us to conform perfectly to the Divine Will as It manifests Its perfect and endless love. In Jesus, God unites His creatures to Himself in a new and more loving way; He shares with us more completely His wisdom and power. He reaches out to us and brings us into perfect harmony with the divine intention of all creation and, thereby, makes us happy, free and eternally alive.

Because this divine mystery of Christ is intended for all, the Church proclaims it to all generations by both word and sacrament which form the basis of the life of faith lived by all its members. When we enter into that mystery through faith, our priorities are changed, our lives are enlarged, and our joy is made full.

Since this immersion into the mystery of Christ is through faith, more is required for growth in Jesus than just receiving the sacraments with accustomed regularity, even the Sacrament of the Holy Eucharist. There is too much evidence of Catholics receiving the sacraments frequently—the Eucharist even daily—without maturing in the mystery of Jesus Christ as their personal Lord and Saviour.

At the same time, there has to be more to the mystery of Christ than just knowing the catechism answers. Most Catholics have received some kind of basic religious education in the catechism; most have some understanding of the fundamental truths of their religion and some awareness of the moral demands that Christianity makes upon the members of Christ's Church. Yet, the majority of practicing Catholics are not noted for having perceptive insights into the mystery of divine wisdom as it reveals itself in the continuing history of the world, the Church and the individual lives of human beings.

As a matter of fact, to simply settle into a comfortable sacramental routine, satisfied with basic catechism knowledge kills true growth in the Lord because the sacraments have meaning only when they flow from faith.

This is not to deny in any way, for example, that the Holy Eucharist is the Body and Blood, Soul and Divinity of Our Lord Jesus Christ through transsubstantiation. Nevertheless, unless, the Eucharist is perceived by the recipient as that Reality, it cannot bear fruit in his life. It is not because the sacrament lacks power to give; rather it is because the recipient lacks faith to receive (Cf. 1 Cor 11:26-32).

The sacraments are *symbolic worship*; they are a liturgical response to the Word of God revealing the mystery of Christ which is heard and rooted deeply in a loving heart. It is faith which creates the environment of the sacraments and enables them to have their full effects, as the *Constitution on the Sacred Liturgy* teaches (#11). Pope Paul VI, in his *Evangelization in the Modern World* assigns this kind of education in faith to evangelization. He writes:

> *The role of evangelization is precisely to educate people in the faith in such a way as to lead each individual Christian to live the Sacraments as true Sacraments of faith—and not to receive them passively or to undergo them* (#47).

In order to grow in the joy and peace that comes from the faith-filled possession of Jesus Christ as Lord and Saviour, it is necessary to grow in the knowledge and appreciation of the word of God, for it is in the word that the dispensation of the mystery of Christ begins.

Growth in the Word of God

There is one way to grow in the word of God which is so obvious that I am surprised that it is so widely overlooked. The obvious way to grow is to read the Bible on a regular basis.

While this seems simple and self-evident, most Catholics, in fact, do not do it. In the past few years of my ministry as a priest, I have been stunned by the number of Catholics who do not read the Scriptures because they actually think it is dangerous to do so.

Not having been educated in the Catholic parochial school system, I have never had the personal experience of being taught that it was either wrong or dangerous to read the Bible. In fact, I have always assumed that Christians should read the Bible, and it has been a delightful lifelong practice of mine. Yet in my ministry, when I have talked to Catholics who have been raised in the Catholic school system, some of them have told me they were specifically warned against reading the Scriptures. The way they describe their educational experiences, it was almost as if they were taught that God wrote the Bible to trick Catholics out of their faith; that if they read the Bible they would give up their faith and become Protestant; that only priests could read the Bible, and even for them it was a risk.

As I listen to them talk, the recurring thought comes to me: if God had wanted to, He could have written a catechism, but the fact of the matter is, the Bible is the word of God, and we are called to take the time, trouble and effort to read it.

Sacred Scripture itself tells of the importance of reading the Bible when Paul writes to Timothy:

> *From (the Scriptures) you can learn the wisdom that leads to salvation through faith in Jesus Christ. All scripture is inspired by God and can profitably be used for teaching, for refuting error, for guiding people's lives and teaching them to be holy. This is how the person dedicated to God becomes fully equipped and ready for any good work* (2 Tm 3:16).

But even with as powerful a quotation from the Bible as that to support the personal study of Scripture, I still have encountered some Catholics who insist that reading the Scriptures is too dangerous to be left up to the individual. I frankly find it impossible to justify or even explain the origins of such a teaching. I have researched the whole area in Church documents rather carefully, and nowhere can I find an official teaching of the Church which discourages the individual Christian from reading the Scriptures as a source of spiritual growth and consolation. The Church has even given indulgences to persons who read the Scriptures for as little as fifteen minutes a day.

The true teaching of the long and venerable tradition of the Church is best summed up in our times in the *Constitution on Divine Revelation* which says:

> *The Church has always venerated the Divine Scriptures just as She venerates the Body of the Lord, since from the table of both the Word of God and the Body of Christ she unceasingly receives and offers to the faithful the bread of life* (#21).

I recently saw the teaching of the Church beautifully symbolized in the arrangement of a small chapel in DeSales High School in Toledo, Ohio. In the center of the chapel was a large altar covered with a white linen cloth. To the left of the altar table the Holy Bible, lying open, was enthroned on a separate stand. To the right of the altar table, on a matching stand, was enthroned the tabernacle with the Holy Eucharist. A vigil candle burned continuously before both the enthroned Bible and the tabernacle, signifying the light of Christ's presence in both Word and Sacrament. This beautiful symbolization of a profound revealed truth led me to lift my heart in praise to God for the greatness of his gifts to us.

Because Christ is present in his word as well as in his sacraments, the Second Vatican Council urged the faithful to read the Scriptures frequently. In this exhortation to frequent reading of the Scriptures, it cited no less an authority than the great St. Jerome himself who lived in the 4th Century and who wrote: "To be ignorant of the Scriptures is to be ignorant of Christ."

If Catholics today are not perceptive with regard to the way God is operating in their daily lives, if they do not appreciate His constant guidance through the gift of the Spirit, if they are not conscious of his shaping them into the image of his beloved Son Jesus Christ, it is because they are not conversant with the Bible. In the Bible God reveals what he is doing for us now—through faith.

Put another way: we cannot really begin to know the mind of Christ unless we know what he says, unless we think his thoughts, share his ideas, strive after his goals and fulfill his aspirations for us. All of the Scriptures are inspired by God, who, through them, wishes to teach us the meaning of our personal as well as communal lives today. As a result, Scriptures are the divine revelation of how much God loves us—now. They are not concerned only with his love of a people in a distant past; rather, through the history of past ages, God reveals his love for us now as a God who is present to us, who has created out of nothing in order that he might share with us his own happiness, his own glory. As Jesus said, "God is the God of the living" (Mt 22:32). The Scriptures, therefore, tell us how we can be happy and, yes, glorious, even though we still dwell in the midst of the valley of the shadow of death.

That strength that comes from the Bible is the strength that comes from the truth. It is the fruit, not of an ideology, but of the experiential knowledge of Three Persons who know us, love us, care for us, and, above all, have the power to make us happy for all eternity. The Sacred Scriptures, being the preaching of God's chosen people written down in the past but directed towards the present, are the marvelous revelation of an Active Mind and a Loving Heart. They constitute the communication of a Mysterious Being who is, and wishes to be, intimately and personally involved with the unfolding of our lives. The Bible, when it is read by believing Christians as a community of faith, casts a new and exciting light on the meaning of our lives today because it reveals the mystery of Christ.

Bible Sharing

Although private reading of the Bible is personally helpful, its ultimate meaning for the human community in terms of salvation is of such importance that it cannot remain a private matter. The good of all demands that the Good News be proclaimed, discussed and witnessed to; in short, the Good News is given to be shared. For example, Paul knew that what he was writing to the Colossians was of such supreme significance for human happiness that it needed to be shared with all. Consequently, he asked the Colossians to share his letter among themselves and then to pass it on to the Laodicians; and at the same time, he wanted the Colossians to get his letter to the Laodicians (Col 4:16). In order to know the meaning of our lives today as God has revealed it through his Scriptures, it is necessary to study the sacred text; we need to become intimately familiar with it so that we can analyze it and arrive at the literal meaning intended by the authors. But, since the Scriptures were written "so that you may believe that Jesus is the Christ, the Son of God, and that believing this you may have life through his name" (Jn 20:31), we cannot stop simply at the study of the surface of the text itself. We must go on to relate the meaning of the text to our own lives so that we can see how God is fulfilling his promises to us in the Scriptures in everything that happens to us.

Whenever anything strikes us in a personal way, we want to share it with someone else. When any experience changes our life or our outlook on life, we have to talk about it. Did you ever visit a friend in the hospital? I would be very surprised if you didn't get every detail of the operation, because what happened to him made a difference.

Man, like God, is a communicator always reaching out to share. Consequently, when the Scriptures strike our hearts and touch our lives so that we appreciate their true relevance to everyday reality, we want to share our understanding of God's word with others. Like a friend's operation, revelation makes a difference. Sharing is the way we really grow in the understanding of the Scriptures. The analytical study of texts is a beginning which is completed through the sharing of personally experienced insights into their meaning for daily life.

We have all had the experience of reading an article in a magazine or newspaper that somehow strikes us as significant, and the first thing we want to do is to read it to someone else to find out if their reaction is the same as ours. We find this kind of reading and sharing a stimulating experience, and as a result of having exchanged views with someone else, we have a new appreciation of what we have read. It could be such a simple thing as sharing the sports page in the newspaper recounting last night's big game which leads to a delightful conversation among friends or it could be as serious as two students going over a complicated homework assignment together as they try to make sense of one of the "great writings."

Richness of Meaning

Since sharing of common experiences is part and parcel of human life, it is not surprising that the sharing of the meaning of the Sacred Scripture is part and parcel of the spiritual life of believing Christians. Because we are delving into divine mystery—the mystery of God's love for us—sharing opens up the depth of meaning each passage contains. Indeed, many passages contain more than one level of meaning, as preachers discover when they preach on the Sunday Scripture texts year after year. You only have to read the various commentaries of the great saints on Scripture to realize that there is no one single statement or proposition that can adequately sum up the fullness of meaning one finds in a gospel parable or a significant story recorded in the Old Testament. As a matter of fact, when we try to propositionalize the parables, by getting rid of the symbol we remove the mystery and destroy the meaning. Who could sum up the parable of the Prodigal Son in a phrase like "God is generous in his mercy" and still preserve its meaning for hearts filled with guilt?

It strikes me strange, therefore, to find that one of the greatest fears I encounter today as I try to encourage Catholics to read the Bible is the fear of "private interpretation." I am not even sure what is meant by the term. Since reading is a self-actualizing dialogue, all of us always have to interpret things we read for ourselves. We necessarily perceive things from the perspectives of our own life, and therefore, have to judge them in the light of our own experience of reality. Nevertheless, after we have arrived at our interpretation, we usually find that other people have arrived at the same understanding, although there will be differences that add spice to our exchange of views and experiences.

An unusually short person experiences human relations rather differently from an exceptionally tall one—talking up is different from talking down. As a result, their practical experience of how to make friends will probably be quite different; still, for all the differences, they will make friends. An even more striking example, of course, is men and women in love. How differently we approach love; yet, who would want to give up the difference?

If this is true of mere human relations, one would expect even greater differences in coming to grips with the profound mystery of God's unfolding love for us. Pope Pius XII himself reassures us concerning this diversity of interpretation in *Divino Afflante Spiritu*, where he writes:

> *There are few texts (in Sacred Scripture) whose sense has been defined by the authority of the Church; nor are those more numerous about which the teaching of the Holy Fathers is unanimous (#47).*

In other words, even the Fathers of the Church found a great variety of richness as their wide range of interpretations show.

At the same time we are especially blessed by being the beneficiaries of the charismatic guidance of the Church promised to us when Jesus said:

*The Advocate, the Holy Spirit, whom the Father will
send in my name, will teach you everything and
remind you of all I have said to you. . . . He will lead
you to the complete truth* (Jn 14:26; 16:13).

The Spirit moves the Church to draw out "new things and old"
from the text He inspired to meet the needs of the changing
times.

The Rejection of Saul

An excellent example of the mystery which the Bible
reveals is found in the story of the rejection of Saul as King of
Israel. The story is recorded in two places with somewhat
different accounts: 1 S 13:8-15 and 1 S 15.

In this story we find that King Saul failed to carry out the
ban against the Amalekites. Although he had been com-
manded by God through the prophet Samuel to annihilate all
the men, women and children of the Amalekites and all their
animals, Saul spared some of the best sheep and oxen in order
to sacrifice them to the Lord God. After Saul had explained to
Samuel his good reason for sparing the animals—in order to
offer sacrifice, Samuel responded:

*Obedience is better than sacrifice and submission
better than the fat of rams. . . . Because you have
rejected the command of the Lord God, He, too, has
rejected you as ruler* (1 S 15:22).

When Saul heard this condemnation of his behaviour, he
immediately admitted his wrong-doing to Samuel crying out:

*I have sinned for I have disobeyed the command of the
Lord God and your instructions. In my fear of the
people I did what they said. Now forgive my sin and
return with me that I may worship the Lord God.*

But Samuel said to Saul:

> *I will not return with you because you rejected the command of the Lord God and the Lord God has rejected you as King of Israel.*

What a shocker that is for us Christians today. In spite of the fact that Saul begged for forgiveness from the Lord through his anointed representative, Samuel, he was refused! As a matter of fact, Scripture seems to indicate that Samuel himself was profoundly upset by God's failure to forgive Saul. We read:

> *The Lord said to Samuel: "How long will you grieve for Saul, whom I have rejected as King of Israel? Fill your horn with oil and be on your way. I am sending you to Jesse of Bethlehem, for I have chosen my king from among his sons"* (1 S 16:1 ff).

The Lord is irritated with His prophet because he mourned over the rejection of Saul.

What a mystery is there! It would be impossible to sum up in any single proposition the significance and meaning of the story of Saul's rejection. Nevertheless, we could discuss it for weeks, and each discussion would bring out another element of the divine mystery we seek so zealously to take hold of in our minds and hearts. What does this story mean for us today? Have we encountered what looks like divine rejection? Can we take forgiveness for granted? How does God bring good out of evil? What are the human consequences of the utterly free divine choice? How important is obedience?

The Parables of the Kingdom

The New Testament is also redolent with mystery. The gospel authors use a variety of literary forms to reveal the meaning of Jesus' life and teaching. Chapter 13 of the Gospel according to Matthew is a particularly rich chapter for Bible sharing since it contains no less than seven different parables, all of which are aimed at communicating the meaning and power of the Kingdom of Heaven.

Jesus, as we know, constantly taught in parables; he probably told many more parables than have come down to us, only the choicest being preserved. It is certain that when he preached, he would draw the stories of the parables out, filling them with rich and touching details. We have, as it were, only a distillation of his preaching, perhaps only the pithy and crucial parts of his lengthy discourses. The same thing happens today, of course; preachers, or teachers in the classroom, talk for many hours, but their listeners remember only the best parts to pass them on or to note them down. So it is the tight succinct phrases of Jesus that have been handed down to us in written form. Since it comes to us through the mind of the sacred writer, we cannot always be sure if we even have Jesus' actual words, but the thought is there, and the teaching is inspired:

> *The reign of God is like a buried treasure which a man found in a field. He hid it again and rejoicing in his find, went and sold all that he had and bought that field* (Mt 13:44).

This means that today we who read the dehydrated preaching of Jesus must mix with it the living waters of the Holy Spirit that come from our own heart where He dwells, guides and teaches us. Gathered together with a group of fellow believers and like-minded Christians, we bring those parables to rich and full life again. They are not just dead sayings of the past, but rather they are entry ways into our own living experience of the Kingdom of God.

The Power to Witness

A good example of how Bible sharing brings to life today the teaching of Jesus in the past centers around the reading of the first chapter of the Acts of the Apostles. There it is recorded how Jesus spent forty days with his very special friends, the apostles, revealing to them the mysteries of the Kingdom. As the story is picked up in Acts, he is about to depart. In order to appreciate the impact their question about the restoration of the Kingdom of Israel must have had on Jesus, we have to recall the circumstances of his life with his apostles.

They were men specially chosen through the Holy Spirit to be with Jesus throughout his ministry on earth; they knew him as no one else did: his daily habits of behaviour, his most intimate thoughts which he shared with them as friends. They saw, moreover, the amazing manifestations of his power, even to raising the dead to life. Three of them had personally seen him transfigured into glory before their very eyes, his clothes changed into a whiteness like a bolt of shimmering lightning, and the divine radiance had overcome them.

These same men saw him under another aspect: a criminal exposed to taunts and ridicule, hanging on a cross; one of their own number having betrayed him to this fate, and the rest fleeing in utter panic at the moment of crisis, one running away with such haste that his would-be captors could grab only his clothes. They were weak men, petty and obtuse and his death left them in despair because they, in spite of everything, loved him.

Now comes a glorious moment in the Scriptures; it almost rivals, in my mind, the Cross as an expression of divine love. In the Gospel of John, the disciples had returned to their fishing business, evidently not knowing what else to do with their lives. Then, at daybreak, Jesus returns to them, guides them to fruitful fishing and prepares breakfast for them. What a magnificent and humbling act of divine forgiveness— forgiveness of weakness and failure. And what that forgiveness meant to the apostles; they picked up where they had been interrupted by death and once again give up all to follow Jesus. Compare this with the rejection of Saul.

Now this is all background for understanding the importance of what we read in the first chapter of Acts because Jesus is about to leave them definitively to return to His Father; this is the last chance they will have to question him directly. So after all they have been through, they ask him what is uppermost in their minds: "Lord, are you going to restore the rule to Israel now?" That is all that they were ultimately concerned about—politics, a Utopia on earth. They wanted the hated Roman conqueror to be overthrown and the kingdom of Israel restored to a glorious earthly reign as seemed to have been promised by so many prophets.

What does Jesus respond at this final moment of truth? He says to them: it's none of your business. Prognostication of the future is not why Jesus became man or called his disciples to fellowship with him. He then makes a solemn statement of purpose which reveals to each of them and to each of us the purpose and meaning of our lives because he says:

> *You will receive power when the Holy Spirit comes down upon you and then you will be my witnesses in Jerusalem, throughout Judea and Samaria; yes, even to the ends of the earth.*

What the apostles received is what we have been given: the power to share in the spreading of the Kingdom of God by bearing personal witness to the risen Lord Jesus; and for that reason he commands us: "Go into the whole world and proclaim the Good News to all creation."

Each one of us, however, will have our own way of carrying out the great commission; each one of us, therefore, experiences the meaning of the first chapter of Acts in different and intensely personal ways. No one interpretation is complete without our actively carrying out the command to bear witness. And this is what Bible sharing does. It enables us to come together with others who have received the Spirit to share our experiences of his power so that together we might grow in our understanding and acceptance of what is revealed through the sacred texts.

We often find our own thinking sharpened and our enthusiasm quickened when we hear someone discuss what we ourselves have read; their remarks put what we have read into a new perspective which leads to a new appreciation of its truth.

So it is with Bible sharing; we learn from the active experience of others what Jesus meant when he said we would become witnesses to him throughout the world. From now on, we will be a little quicker in working for the Gospel because we realize our very identity as Christians is intimately tied up with the growth of the Church. Therefore, the history of the early Church throughout the whole Acts of the Apostles becomes particularly relevant to us, because now it is our history as well, a history still being enacted in our own day—Gospel history because we live in Gospel power.

CHAPTER THREE

BIBLE SHARING AS A MEANS OF GROWTH

We are fortunate to be living in these times because today we know more about the Bible, or at least have the resources to know more about the Bible, than any other people at any other time in the past. We live in the age of "The Great Explosion" when it comes to biblical scholarship. Since 1950 especially, but also in the twenty years preceding it, scriptural research has plunged forward as the result of an amazing multiplication of tools and discoveries. Archeologists, for example, are able to reconstruct lost civilizations that exerted tremendous influence on the peoples of the Bible. As recently as the last decade, archeologists discovered in the desert sands of Northern Syria an advanced and extensive city-state that flourished 2500 years ago. Forty-thousand cuneiform tablets found in the royal archives of Ebla tell us of the daily life, commerce, education, politics and religion of a people that antedated the peoples recorded in the oldest biblical records and who might well have been the forbearers of the Hebrew patriarchs. Indeed, the very name *Hebrew* is related to a proper name of that civilization, and in their pantheon of gods, the Eblaites honored the god Yah. Is the name of Yahweh a derivative of that?

As a result of discoveries like this, we have a new comprehension, as yet still only beginning to be developed, of the cultures in the Bible: how they were formed, where they came from. Scholars can reconstruct with amazing accuracy how the Bible itself came to be written and compiled because of their new familiarity with the people and the cultures that gave it birth. We can also check on the reliability of the way the Bible has been transmitted to us down through the centuries. In 1947, archeologists discovered ancient Jewish texts that had laid undisturbed for 2000 years at Qumran which give us a totally new appreciation of the accuracy of the Hebrew biblical texts we have been using since the 10th century, A.D.

Nor do these fruits of research remain hidden in remote monasteries or carefully locked libraries which give access only to a few chosen scholars. Cheap printing processes make the finest of biblical research and archeological investigation readily available to all. Go into a good book store, and you will find shelf after shelf of biblical resource materials ranging from expensive hardback books to inexpensive paper pamphlets, and now we are also finding the fruits of scholarship reflected in visual and audio-visual materials. Each item is geared for different needs, yet all reflect the finest fruits of biblical scholarship.

Mercifully Simple

For all the richness and complexity of the resources available to us today resulting from the scholarship explosion in biblical studies, Bible sharing as a means of growing in Jesus is remarkably simple. Only three things are really necessary: a good Bible, believing people and the Holy Spirit. These three come together in a regular program of meetings in which the revelation of God found in His Holy Bible is discussed by the people of God under the guidance of the Holy Spirit so that each participant may grow in a personal awareness and appreciation of God's saving action in his life through the Lord Jesus.

A Good Bible

There are two editions of the Bible which I personally recommend: The first is the *Jerusalem Bible*. Admittedly the translation while euphonious is not the best available for study;

however, there is no other single Bible that has such fine introductions to the individual books and such excellent and plentiful footnotes. Unfortunately, the completely annotated volume is published only in hardback or leather. The paperback edition, the very popular *Reader's Edition*, does not contain all the footnotes of the more expensive versions, and the real value of the *Jerusalem Bible* is in its introductions and footnotes. For example, it would be very hard for anyone to read Paul's *Letter to the Romans* as it is annotated in the *Jerusalem Bible* and arrive at a "private interpretation" that is not in accord with orthodox Christian teaching. In addition, the *Jerusalem Bible* has cross-references conveniently arranged down the side of each page which help the reader to immediately locate other places in the Bible where the same topic, thought or theme is expressed. For instance, a marginal note alongside Rm 7:1 refers the reader to Gal 2:19 which also speaks of the Law and the life of faith. Because the *Jerusalem Bible* was edited under Catholic auspices (the Dominican *Ecole Biblique* in Jerusalem), it contains all the books of the Canon recognized by the Catholic Church as well as the more limited Old Testament Canon accepted by the Protestant Churches.

A second Bible I highly recommend for Bible sharing is *The New American Bible*. While *The New American Bible* also has excellent footnotes and introductions, they are not as complete or profound as those in the *Jerusalem Bible*. However, the footnotes and introductions, unlike those in the *Jerusalem Bible*, are found in all editions of *The New American Bible* including the less expensive paperback editions. It also has cross-references which appear at the bottom of the pages, but these can be quite confusing if one is not used to reading cross-references. *The New American Bible* translation is the one used in most Catholic lectionaries for the Eucharistic liturgy. In fact it is widely used in all the sacramental liturgies, since no sacrament is to be celebrated without readings from the word of God.

Both of these Bibles have another feature which is particularly helpful to those not yet familiar with reading the

Scriptures: the editors have broken up the text into various divisions, each having a heading or subheading which describes the subject matter of the section. Such a procedure helps the reader to organize his reading of the Bible so that the meaning fairly leaps out from the printed page. Without such divisions, one can become confused because sometimes the transitions in the texts themselves are not that clear. Having the divisions is like having a teacher point out to you the direction the text is going and what it intends to say.

There are, of course, many other excellent editions of the Holy Bible put out under both Catholic and Protestant auspices. An outstanding Protestant Bible is the *Revised Standard Version*, available from the American Bible Society. It is basically an up-dating of the *King James Version*, the result of a number of revisions, which uses modern English while preserving something of the flavor of the *King James Version*. Because it uses an excellent manuscript tradition closely akin to the one used by the *Latin Vulgate*, this translation has the merit of combining what is probably the most accurate translation available in English with a literary style that has a pleasant ring of familiarity to both Catholics and Protestants. Unlike the other two editions discussed, however, the *Revised Standard Version* lacks footnotes and divisions; as a result, it can be more difficult for beginners to appreciate.

A fourth edition which is very popular today is the Good News Bible. For some time it was available only for the New Testament and was known as *Good News for Modern Man*. Now the Old Testament has also been made available, and together they make up the *Good News Bible*. This is an easy translation to read because it limits itself to words which would be found in a daily newspaper; while easy to read, it may not fully communicate the subtleness of thought in the original languages because of the limited vocabulary.

There are, of course, many other versions of the Bible, more than can reasonably be discussed here. Two versions, however, should be used only with considerable caution: *The Living Bible* and *The Way*. In fact, they cannot really be classified as Bibles because they are not translations of the Sacred Text, but rather paraphrases of it which are the product of theological reflection. They try to summarize the thought of the original and to clarify it for today's reader. The result is not the word of God but the word of man as he reflects and interprets the word of God. While such books can be very helpful in understanding the meaning of Scripture, it is important to realize that they are not Scripture itself.

All members of the Bible sharing groups need not use the same translation. As a matter of fact, Bible sharing can be greatly enhanced when different translations are used. There is a sense of excitement, challenge and interest generated when differing translations of the same passage are compared. A stimulating discussion can quickly grow out of the fact that different translators see two different emphases in the text and use different English words to bring out basically the same and therefore inspired meaning.

Believing People

The second thing that is needed for fruitful Bible sharing is the gathering together of believing Christians. Because the Bible is written for those who already believe in Jesus Christ, it is not the time to engage in defensive debates about the person, nature or power of Him whom we acknowledge as our Lord and Saviour; it is a time for sharing faith-given insights into the meaning of His Lordship for us today as revealed in the Bible. The Spirit that draws Bible sharers together is not the spirit of controversy and correction; it is the Spirit of loving exchange. It is not the time for acrimonious argument about past historical wrongs or misunderstandings, nor is it the time for investigating doctrinal errors.

Bible sharers come together out of a sincere desire to grow in their understanding of the word of God and appreciation of the powerful love of Jesus. They come together with an eager willingness to listen to one another respectfully, treasuring each other's insights and experiences, and at the same time, with an eager desire to share personal experiences of revealed truth in their lives. Freedom of thought, reverence of expression and equality of views are essential for fruitful Bible sharing where the Bible itself is the rule of faith.

This is not to deny differences of belief, especially in our tragically divided Christianity; but these differences bring out the richness of the mystery revealed in the Scriptures. Exchange of views about these differing traditions can enhance our understanding of our own all-embracing tradition and, at the same time, help us to see the complexity of the Christian life and enable us to respect the traditions of others. When important—that is, fundamental—doctrinal definitions are involved, the Catholic Bibles I have recommended will have footnotes that can guide you to a fully orthodox understanding of the words of Scripture. (For example, in the *Jerusalem Bible* see footnote *j* in Rm 1:17 which discusses rather completely the orthodox understanding of faith). When difficulties persist, of course, there are a plethora of resource materials available to which we should turn. Parish libraries should have them easily accessible; if they do not, the Bible sharing group itself should build up a resource library for its members.

Bible sharing, therefore, is not a time of Bible teaching; that can be done elsewhere. The principles that govern fruitful Bible sharing exclude one or another member of the group from being the teacher, prophet, preacher or evangelizer. While it is important for each to bear personal witness to his experience of the word of God in his life, it is the kind of witness that is born of the full appreciation that the word operates in other peoples' lives as well; consequently, whatever testimony is given is shared testimony and not an imposed "you listen while I talk because I really know what the truth is." Nothing can kill true Bible sharing faster than having one member take over and dominate the group with witness and ready answers. A very important part of dynamic Bible sharing is an eager listening in respectful silence.

The Fundamental Principle of Sharing

At the same time, no one can fruitfully participate in Bible sharing by remaining silent all the time. You cannot expect to be a sponge, absorbing information without revealing your own experiences, values and ideas. Bible sharing is based on the fundamental principle that when groups of Christians come together and openly exchange with one another in honest, loving equality their faith-filled insights into the meaning of Sacred Scripture, this exchange of insights among believers with diverse personalities and from varied backgrounds will itself be productive of new and more profound insights into the significance of what God has revealed.

Clearly, therefore, Bible sharing is not a substitute for Bible study. On the contrary, it both presupposes and builds on Bible study. For rewarding Bible sharing, it is necessary for members of the group to come to each session well-prepared: each having read the Scripture itself, studied the introduction and footnotes, and even, when possible, having consulted other resource materials. Each should have a fairly well developed opinion of what the passage to be discussed is saying. This will probably be modified in the course of the discussion, but at least each should start with a fairly clear notion of the message as he understands it in the light of his own faith experience. Bible sharing without Bible study is simply pooled ignorance.

On the other hand, Bible sharing goes beyond Bible study because the group does not stop with the literal meaning which is only the surface explanation of the passage. Rather, it extends itself to come to grips with the meaning of the Scriptures for our spiritual life today. It finds the meaning of Scripture today through the making of personal decisions about the priorities of life and love. As Jesus said:

> *It is not those who say to me, "Lord, Lord," who will enter into the kingdom of heaven, but the person who does the will of my Father in heaven* (Mt 7:21).

We will have more to say about this important principle in Chapter Eight, when we also give specific guidelines for forming Bible sharing groups.

The Holy Spirit and the Words of Life

Finally what is required for effective Bible sharing is the presence of the Holy Spirit. It is through the Holy Spirit that the Bible was written, and it is only in the Holy Spirit that we can hear the full message of the Bible and enter into the mystery of Christ. Prayer, therefore, is an essential component of Bible sharing. Each session should begin with prayer, end in prayer and be salted with prayer. Stopping in the midst of a discussion about a difficult passage to invoke the Holy Spirit is the best way of assuring that the total meaning will shine forth with new clarity and relevance. Therefore, while study is important, prayer is equally important. Study and sharing both should be done in the prayerful recognition that when we share the word of God we are not exchanging views of secular truth but are striving to penetrate deeply into the meaning of divine wisdom. Prayer enables us to be continually aware that no matter how great the insights we have, we can never fully encompass or appreciate the word of God since it is the word of eternal life.

Speaking of Jesus, who gives us the word of eternal life, Pope Pius XII concluded his landmark encyclical on the study of Sacred Scripture, *Divino Afflante Spiritu*, with the words that should be written in the hearts of all who share the Bible:

> *To Our most merciful Redeemer we must therefore bring back all by every means in our power. For, He is the Divine Consoler of the afflicted. He it is Who teaches all, whether they be invested with public authority or are bound in duty to obey and submit, true honest, absolute justice and generous charity. It is He, in the end, and He alone who can be the firm foundation and support of peace and tranquility: "For other foundation no man can lay, but that which is*

laid: which is Christ Jesus." Thus, the author of salvation, Christ, will men fully know, more ardently love and more faithfully imitate in proportion as they are more assiduously urged to know and meditate on Scripture, especially the New Testament. As St. Jerome, the patron of biblical studies says: "To ignore the Scripture is to ignore Christ:" and again: "If there is anything in this life which sustains a wise man and induces him to maintain his serenity amidst the tribulations and adversities of the world, it is in the first place, I consider, the meditation and knowledge of the Scriptures."

There, those who are wearied and oppressed by adversities and afflictions will find true consolation and divine strength to suffer and bear with patience; there—that is in the Holy Gospels—Christ, the highest and greatest example of justice, charity and mercy, is present to all; and to the lacerated and trembling human race are laid open the foundations of that divine grace without which both peoples and their rulers can never arrive at, never establish, peace in the state and unity of heart; there, in the end, all will learn Christ, "Who is the head of all principality and power" and "who of God is made unto us wisdom and justice and sanctification and redemption" (Divino Afflante Spiritu, #57, #58).

CHAPTER FOUR

CHARACTERISTICS OF THE BIBLE AS THE WORD OF GOD

A common mistake is to think of the Bible as a single book. It is not. The Bible is really an extensive anthology, a collection of disparate writings; it might best be described as a library of sacred pamphlets. Indeed, as you begin to read the Bible regularly perhaps the most striking thing about it is the many diverse kinds of literature it contains: prose and poetry; history and legend; philosophical musings, prophetic proclamations; letters, stories, gospels. We can be misled into thinking of it as a single book, which starts on the first page and ends on the last, because we usually read all these different literary masterpieces in one bound volume with its pages consecutively numbered and printed in a uniform type style.

Nevertheless, for all the diversity of its origins, a composition spanning ten centuries and as many different stages of cultural development, written by men of vastly different temperaments, personalities and backgrounds, the Bible does have a unique unity: it contains the revelation of God. Through His Holy Bible, the Creator of the entire universe and everything in it reveals to those whom He has chosen the depths of His wisdom, His knowledge and His love. The Father of Being reveals to His children that he is more than a blind creative force operating according to fixed laws of nature; He is a free Being Who thinks and loves and Who wishes to have us always in His Presence.

What the Bible reveals, then, is an ongoing relationship between the Creator of all things and His creatures, the Father and His children. It describes a relationship which, while it begins on earth, will only be completed in eternity, and it is a relationship of power, knowledge and love which brings the creature to completion, fulfillment and joy:

> *We know that anyone who has been begotten by God does not sin, because the begotten Son of God protects him, and the Evil One does not touch him. We know that we belong to God, but the whole world lies in the power of the Evil One. We know, too, that the Son of God has come, and has given us the power to know the true God. We are in the true God, as we are in His Son, Jesus Christ. This is the true God, this is eternal life* (1 Jn 5:18-20).

In this chapter we will explore the characteristics of the Bible that enable us to say with such confidence that the Bible is the word of God. We will explain the relationship between human authorship and human culture and divine authorship and eternal truth. We will also consider how it came about that the Church could recognize the books of the Bible as divine revelation. Such an explanation is important today because of contemporary controversies over the "inerrancy" of the Scripture. We will show in what sense Scripture can be said to be free of all error.

Inspiration

The principal author of revelation is none other than God himself who, by the powerful action of the Holy Spirit, moved human writers to write in a way which revealed the Divine Mystery. While there are many different opinions, theories and explanations of how inspiration takes place, all who accept the Bible as the revealed word of God agree on this: that using human authors with diverse talents and temperaments (some optimistic by nature, others surprisingly gloomy pessimists) Almighty God so perfectly controlled their creative act of writing that what they produced—products of their own time, circumstances, culture and personality—can be said to be, and in truth is, the word of God. Furthermore, it is precisely this action of the Holy Spirit, spanning so many centuries and circumstances, which gives a profound inner cohesion to all of the Holy Bible. Ultimately, inspiration took place to reveal the person and message of Jesus Christ through whom you and I are rescued from our sins and given eternal life through faith.

> *At various times in the past and in various different ways, God spoke to our ancestors through the prophets; but in our own time, the last days, He has spoken to us through His son, the Son that He has appointed to inherit everything and through whom He made everything there is. He is the radiant light of God's glory and the perfect copy of His nature, sustaining the universe by His powerful command; and now that He has destroyed the defilement of sin, He has gone to take his place in heaven at the right hand of Divine Majesty* (Heb 1:1-4).

The Holy Scriptures, therefore, contain profound mystery which can be known and revealed only by the Spirit of God. The Holy Spirit penetrates into the very depths of God's understanding of Himself and us. No human authors could ever fully write about the Divine Essence; no human mind could come close to knowing the fullness of the Divine mind. Yet, what the authors have captured is what God wishes to reveal to us about Himself in order that through faith we might accept His word, experience its power, grow in obedience to it, and ultimately, share it with others.

The Sacred Canon

Because the Holy Bible was written by the Holy Spirit in such a way that it is the word of God, it can only be appreciated and understood as the word of God if it is read in the Holy Spirit. Those 73 special books, which are the word of God in a unique way constitute what is known as the Canon of Scripture or Rule of Faith. Over the centuries, the Jewish people, and later the Christian Church as well, recognized certain books of their holy literature as inspired by God; they acknowledged some books they read as uniquely holy, a special address from God to His people. The Christian Church also recognized that certain works which they were using in their liturgical celebrations were the result of God's special action in the hearts and minds of the writers. Not all the writings used in the liturgies of either the Jewish or Christian religions contained this inspired quality, only those that survived the test of faith.

The first group of sacred writings constitute what we have come to term the Old Testament, while the inspired writings of the Christian dispensation are called the New Testament; together, they make up the revelation of God.

> *The books of Scripture must be acknowledged as teaching firmly, faithfully, and without error that truth which God wanted to put into the sacred writings for the sake of our salvation* (Div. Rev. #11).

As a result, all the preaching of the Church flows from and is nourished by the Sacred Scriptures. The Holy Bible as it is passed down through the successive centuries by the preaching of the Christian Church Universal is the supreme rule of faith. The *Dogmatic Constitution on Divine Revelation* of the Second Vatican Council gives the reason for the Church's insistence that its veneration of the Divine Scriptures is comparable to its veneration of the Body of the Lord:

> *For in the sacred books, the Father Who is in heaven meets His children with great love and speaks with them; and the force and power in the Word of God is so great that it remains the support and energy of the Church, the strength of faith for her sons, the food of the soul, the pure and perennial source of spiritual life* (Div. Rev. #21).

That God Himself should reveal His mind to His creatures is wonderful indeed. It is something the dimensions of which can only be appreciated by those who have faith. Because through His word we become more than servants, we become friends of God, divine revelation is a unique event in human history and a marvelous manifestation of the divine condescension. On the other hand, it is not magic.

Christian revelation does not depend on a magical finding of golden tablets written by angel hands or on secret documents handed down in sacred rituals which are open only to an elite corp of initiates. On the contrary, God speaks to all of us, His children, in a very human way because God is a marvelous craftsman who respects His own handiwork. Respecting His handiwork, God shapes, molds, and brings to completion the human person through the revelation of His loving will in a way which is always in accord with human nature: through the agency of human preachers and writers. Since the Bible is the manifestation of the Divine Mind showing the operation of the Divine Being in reality today, the Bible is divine. At the same time, the Bible is also intensely and completely human because each and every page reflects the personalities, the times, the circumstances, the prejudices, the ignorance, the brilliance and the genius of its human authors.

Human Authorship

In order to appreciate the magnificence of God's inspirational activity, it is important to take a closer look at those men whom He inspired. Who are they? When you research the subject as preparation for Bible sharing, you will find it in most resource books under the title, "authenticity," the area of research which tries to solve the problems arising from human authorship: did the person to whom the book is attributed actually write it? For example, did Moses himself write the *Pentateuch*, the first five books of the Bible? From things that Jesus said, it would seem that Jesus thought he did. Or again, did David write all the psalms he is credited with? Was there only one Isaiah who wrote the whole book of Isaiah?

At first, it might seem that identifying who the human authors of the Bible are is not very important, since we know that whoever they are God inspired them so that whatever they wrote, it is His word, and that is the only thing that matters. However, as we grow in the reading of the word of God, we discover that who wrote the various books really does make a difference in trying to understand what God wants to reveal. For, if our research leads to the discovery that the authors are not really the ones tradition has said they are, we have a big problem. If, for instance, Moses did not really write *Deuteronomy* (and scholars say he did not), can we trust anything that is written in the Bible, because the Bible itself says that Moses wrote *Deuteronomy*. In other words, the problems associated with authenticity or authorship can seem to call into question the reliability and inerrancy of the Sacred Scriptures and, hence, their value as divine revelation and guides to Christian belief and life.

It is not the purpose of this book to go into an extensive study of authenticity since so many books are available on the subject. Nevertheless, I would like to point out a few perspectives that can help Bible sharers to appreciate more fully the artistry of God in writing the Bible to reveal His heart and mind to us.

Ways of Being an Author

There are a number of different ways one can be said to be author. We are very familiar with some of them today, but others are not so easily recognized. In fact, we would not call some people authors who are called authors by the writers of the Bible. It is a cultural difference which we have to learn to appreciate if we are going to be able to value what authorship of the Bible books means.

First, someone who sits down at a table and writes a book with his own hand word-for-word is obviously the author. Some of the books of the Bible were probably written like this; for example, the *Gospel According to Luke*. Luke tells his readers how he devoted himself to examining all the existing traditions about Jesus and putting them together in order so that Theophilus, the man for whom he was writing, could see for himself the reasonableness of his faith—that it was founded on a real person and real incidents.

In other cases, however, the author did not write the book himself; he dictated it to others. For example, Paul dictated his great *Letter to the Romans* to Tertius who was the one who actually wrote it; yet, it is certainly Paul's letter (Cf. Rm 16:22). Paul dictated other letters as well and was content with simply signing his name in his own hand to what he had dictated.

Sometimes authorship is a bit more complicated because we are not in tune with the custom of attributing books to people who did not write them; on the other hand, in all honesty, many political speeches are really written by "ghost writers," while they are given by a politician as if they were his own. In this way, the ideas in the speech gain the authority and prestige of the political leader to whom they are attributed instead of coming from an unknown speech writer.

There is something analogous to this kind of authorship in the Bible. For example, some of the *Psalms of David* were not written by David at all, but whoever did write them attributed them to David because David was a man of God and of music, and the author wanted his psalms to have something of David's prestigious authority.

A better example of this kind of acceptable use of authorship is found in the *Book of Wisdom* or the *Wisdom of Solomon* as it is known in the Greek. Although this book was actually written centuries after King Solomon, it was attributed to him because Solomon was the personification of wisdom—a man specially endowed by God with the gift of discerning judgment. Since Solomon never had the chance to accept or reject authorship of this work, we moderns feel a little uncomfortable about such attribution; the ancients, on the other hand, did not share our sensitivity.

There is a final type of authorship we do feel more at home with. Some of the books in the Bible, for example, *Isaiah*, or *Jeremiah* or even the *Gospel According to John* were actually authored by their disciples, men who were steeped in the ideas of their master and their ways of thinking to such an extent that what they put into writing were accurate reflections of their teacher's thought, and the resulting books were harmonious developments of the master's original preaching. It might be compared to a college student studying diligently under one of his professors and then authoring a book that was basically a compilation of his professor's classroom notes. Today we demand that the student publish it under his own name, giving credit to his professor for the basic ideas, but we would not tolerate his publishing it under the professor's name. This, however, is a modern nicety which did not govern the practice of the biblical writers. Incidentally, if the student did not credit his professor with the ideas, we would call it plagiarism.

Diverse Times, Diverse Cultures

Our discussion about authorship is important, if somewhat confusing, for another reason than simply trying to maintain the inerrancy of the Sacred Scriptures. Fruitful sharing of the Holy Bible cannot take place unless we appreciate the diverse theologies that are reflected in the different books which were written at different times by different people. In fact, such are the extremes of theological positions included in the Bible that at times one book might seem to contradict what is written in another. You have often heard the expression: "You can make Scripture say anything you want. Even the devil can quote Scripture to support himself."

That is simply not true. All the teachings of the Bible must be considered before we can arrive at the full meaning of any single section or book because the Holy Spirit has provided His masterpiece with an inner unity that actually comes about because of the diversity it contains. Let me illustrate what I mean.

Probably the earliest actual writing down of any part of the entire Holy Bible occurred with the sections which comprise what biblical scholars call the Yahwistic (J) tradition of the *Pentateuch* as the first five books of the Old Testament are called. This tradition is identifiable from the fact that it uses the Mosaic name of God, *Yahweh,* instead of another name for God, *Elohim.* These Yahwistic sections were committed to writing perhaps as early as the tenth century before Christ; yet, even these early writings reach back still further into time because they contain oral traditions which were popular among the people in the eleventh to thirteenth centuries before Christ. In other words, the unknown yet divinely inspired authors of the earliest sections of the Sacred Scriptures record for us the stories, the legends, the traditions of a primitive, nomadic people who reflected on and tried to come to grips with the odyssey they had undertaken in faith. Even these early sections reflect the people's understanding of a God Who had made a promise to their patriarch Abraham and manifest their complete confidence that He would make Abraham a great leader and the father of nations. (Actually, newly-emerging evidence indicate that these early people and their ideas might not be as primitive as some had previously thought).

Note, while the earliest writings found in the *Pentateuch* are dated to the tenth century, B.C., the entire first five books of the Old Testament, were not put into the form with which we are familiar until the fourth century, B.C., or 600 years later. When they were finally put into the present form, the earliest writings had been extensively edited and combined with later written and oral traditions. Biblical scholars, called exegetes, who have dedicated their lives to the scientific and scholarly understanding of the Sacred Scriptures are today able to accurately isolate the different traditions which make up the *Pentateuch.* Nevertheless, the complexity of its origins have resulted in serious difficulties for Christians over the course of time.

To cite just one of many examples: sincere Christians are bitterly divided over the meaning and purpose of the creation stories. Some are deeply convinced that these stories must be taken literally. If it says six days for creation, it took six days; others dismiss the whole story of creation as nothing more than myth, with no foundation in reality. In order to have the proper perspective to judge these opposing viewpoints, Bible sharers need to pursue further the study of the composition of the Bible. The topic will be found in good biblical commentaries under the title of *form criticism* and *redaction criticism.* While it takes a bit of work, study also makes us want to praise God more fully as we come to appreciate the wonderful way He revealed Himself to us through the agency of so many human authors over such a long span of time. What a credit to His power and love!

On the other hand, since the *Book of Genesis* is so complicated it would be a mistake for beginners in Bible sharing to start their sharing sessions with it. Instead, Bible sharers should begin with the New Testament, always reading the sections of the Old Testament that are referred to in the New Testament passages they are reading, until such time as they have developed sufficient background to appreciate the different cultures and conditions which gave birth to the Old Testament. There is definitely a time to read the Old Testament, since, after all, it is the revelation of God. However, that is not the best starting point for Christian readers.

With regard to the question we raised at the beginning of this section: Did Moses write the *Pentateuch?* The answer is: yes, he wrote it. Not in the sense of personal authorship, not in the sense that he sat down at a desk and wrote it with his own hand. Moses is the author of *Pentateuch* because he is the great religious leader who stands at the absolute center of the *Pentateuch* and who brought the people into being as a people.

Without him, there would be no *Pentateuch*, and so the *Pentateuch* ultimately rests on the authority of Moses, the great Prophet of the Lord Most High.

The New Testament and the Apostolic Presence

The New Testament was the product of the early Christian community's cumulative efforts to preserve the apostolic presence in both time and space. When they were absent, the apostles would write letters to their own communities or to other cummunites, as did Paul for example. When it became clear that Christ would not soon return on the clouds of heaven signaling the end of the world, the Christian communities began to write down the preaching of the apostles so that their witness and teaching would be preserved even after their deaths.

While most Scripture scholars agree that the New Testament books were all written between 47 and 125 A.D., in a very recent study—*Re-dating the New Testament*—which is still being hotly debated, the Anglican Bishop, Dr. John A.T. Robinson proposes the thesis that the entire New Testament was written before the fall of Jerusalem in 70 A.D. His principle argument is that if the fall of Jerusalem had taken place before the New Testament was written, such a critical event in the life of Judeo-Christian community would have been at least mentioned, and it is not.

Yet, no matter how brief the interval during which the New Testament was composed, the different books of the New Testament reflect the existence of a remarkable diversity of theological viewpoints and traditions in the young Church. Unless the Bible sharer appreciates the richness of experience implicit in such diversity of expression, he might overlook, disregard, or worse, deny the very real differences that exist in the various writings.

For example, compare St. Paul's view of justification by faith in relation to works in *Romans* (3:21-4:25) to that of *James'* (Jm 2:14-26). Or for a more vivid example, consider the differences in Paul's own viewpoints concerning the end-times: Compare his vindictive, violent description of the Christian victory in *2 Thessalonians* (1:6-12) with his quite, calm and praise-filled description of the all-embracing mystery of Christ in *Ephesians* (3:1-21).

Sometimes, on the other hand, one book of the Bible expands on or summarizes the ideas contained in another. So, while the *Gospel of John* (3:15) states that life comes through faith, *Galatians* (3:1-9) clarifies for us what that life of faith entails, and even gives us practical norms for us to judge how faithfully we are actually living (5:16-26). These norms, of course, are only Paul's theological development of Jesus' pithy saying: "By their fruits you shall know them" (Cf. Mt 7:15-23). Finally, the *First Letter of John* shows the relationship of the power of God in us to its fruits, its good works (3:6-10).

Far from being upset, therefore, at the seeming contradictions and divergencies so apparent in the Bible, the Christian who appreciates the way the Bible was compiled will realize anew the limitations of human learning and communication and will devote himself to the delightful, but at times arduous, task of sifting out the various traditions in order to arrive at what is the focus of them all—Jesus Christ in power and glory!

CHAPTER FIVE

THE VARIETY OF FORMS IN BIBLICAL LITERATURE

In addition to having been written over many centuries by many different authors, reflecting many different theological and cultural orientations, the Bible also is made up of a variety of literary forms, each one of which must be appreciated on its own terms if its meaning is to be truly grasped in faith. We cannot just pick up the Holy Bible and read it like we would the daily newspaper, or as a personal love letter from God to me whose words I should accept just as they pop out from the page "in the Spirit." To read the Bible in this simplistic way, I need only a good English dictionary and a prayer, but, then, I do not really enter into the revealed mystery.

An extreme example of this mentality is found in people who "cut" the Bible to find meaning for their lives. That is, they simply utter a prayer and then open the Bible at random; the first passage they light on is what God intends to tell them for that day or to solve that crisis. Whether they read a passage from Isaiah or the Psalms or St. John does not really matter; the important thing is the brief passage their fingers fall on. This is God's message to them. It is also magic and superstition, and we do like magic.

Unfortunately, in spite of our penchant for magical solutions, nothing could be more harmful to long-range, personal growth in the Lord Jesus. Meaning comes to us not only through inidividual words, sentences and passages; meaning comes to us through the structure of the book and the literary form of the passage which the writer selected as the best way of communicating the truth God had inspired him to write. So to get at meaning, we need to appreciate form and structure. We need to be sensitive to the intention of the author in writing a particular passage of the Bible, since this will determine the literary form in which he expresses himself. Does he communicate his thought through fact or fiction, prose or poetry, satire or polemic? How are the various parts arranged to bring out the central meaning he intends? Does he use the structure of epic poem, a play or an historical record? Each literary type of writing has its own rules and principles of composition and interpretation which we need to respect if we are ever to attain the truth each contains.

Although we probably do not think about it, we do this all the time when we come to grips with modern forms of communication. A business man does not read an office memo the same way he reads a love letter from his wife; we do not look for the same kind of truth in a newspaper advertisement as we do in a straight news story. We read the editorial page with a different, if unconscious, expectation than we do the front page; and a detective story does not have to stand the same discriminating judgment we exercise when reading the great American novel. More and more we find fact and fiction are melted together as one in "documentaries," and television "news" has become theatre.

Furthermore, we sometimes come closer to truth through insightfully written fiction than we do through factual reporting. Vital statistics do not reveal as much about a person as a good anecdote which may or may not have actually taken place. Each family has its legends about Mom's or Dad's childhood that accurately reveal the person but do violence to the facts. "Dad, it doesn't snow in Florida; you couldn't have walked to school in the snow!" Yet, the energy to walk through the snow—had it been there—is real and persists even to the day of the child who has to listen for the umpteenth time to the stories about the old days when things were really tough, like going to school in the snow.

It exceeds the purpose of this book to go into an extended description of the various literary forms found in the Bible. The reader can find many excellent books written at different levels of complexity which provide rather complete treatments of literary forms; such readings are a part of the serious and continuing preparation necessary for fruitful Bible sharing.

Here it is enough to point out some of the forms used by the writers of both Old and New Testaments in order to appreciate the fact that the Bible uses a multiplicity of literary types to communicate the Word of God: history, prophecy, legend, poetry, sermon, letter and gospel.

History

A great part of the Old Testament is obviously the story of the old days. The history of Israel is written recounting of a people's journey into faith; the development of a primitive, nomadic tribe of wanderers, loosely organized and endlessly at war, into a nation of stable, independent people with cities, nobles and kings. It is the story, too, of a fallen nation, conquered, exiled, dispersed, yet miraculously delivered from bondage and filled with an incredible hope and trust in One God, the Creator of all things. It is the formation of God's chosen people, who, no matter what befalls them, know that God has singled them out from among all peoples in order that He might show to them the fullness of His special love.

Prophecy

While the historical form used in the Scriptures seeks to interpret the meaning of the things that happened to this people to show how God is always with His people as their Rock and their Salvation, the prophetic form allows a more direct expression of this Divine Presence. It allows God to speak not just in events but as a person through the mouth of specially appointed spokesmen—the prophets. So, for example, through the Prophet Isaiah, the Lord God speaks to His chosen people and says:

You, Israel, my servant,
Jacob whom I have chosen,
descendant of Abraham my friend.

You whom I brought from the confines of the earth
and called from the ends of the world;
you to whom I said, 'You are my servant,
I have chosen you, not rejected you,'
do not be afraid, for I am with you;
stop being anxious and watchful for I am your God...

But you yourself still rejoice in Yahweh,
and glory in the Holy One of Israel (Is 41:8-10, 16).

Legend

Furthermore, since God's relationship to His creatures goes back to the beginning, the first eleven chapters of *Genesis* do not limit themselves to history but reach back even further into prehistoric time, even to when the earth was a "formless void," even before there was a man or woman to know, much less to report. The Bible begins, fittingly enough, with the beginning when God made the heavens and the earth. The inspired writers reveal these times through myths and legends which, nevertheless, reveal, under divine inspiration, the most profound truth of all—everything comes from the One God of Israel, and it is all good. It is only later, God teaches us, that the evil we experience so constantly in our lives comes into being, marring the beauty of God's original creation; yet, it is an evil which God's people will overcome through faith in Jesus.

Poetry

In addition to sacred history, prophecy and legend, God's truth comes to us through the sacred songs and poems which make up a great part of the Old Testament. The most obvious grouping is the collection found in the *Book of Psalms*, sacred songs which beautifully express God's relationship to man. Sometimes this relationship is revealed in terms of temple worship, at other times the revelation comes through the secret anguish of the poet's heart. Some songs are like our liturgical chants and hymns today; others are more like popular folk-songs which comment on the meaning of life. Nor are these relevatory songs limited to the *Book of Psalms*. We find them scattered throughout the pages of the Old Testament in *Jeremiah, Isaiah, Judges*; as a result, we cannot think of even one book as containing only a single literary form.

Sermons

We find sermons scattered everywhere throughout both the Old and New Testaments, and a sermon cannot be read the same way as anything else because wherever it is found, a sermon is still a sermon and follows its own rules. Some sermons are rather highly developed, like some of *Isaiah* and *Amos*; others are only recorded through brief notes so that we have difficulty in reconstructing the original presentation. This is particularly true of the preaching of Jesus himself, where, as noted before, hours of his preaching are recorded in only a few memorable lines.

The Letters of Paul

The letters of St. Paul to his various Christian communities, friends and pastoral associates present a particular challenge to us today. While we have become used to a rather systematic presentation of religious truths in academically respectable forms of writing which can withstand the rigid scrutiny of logic, such is not the custom of Paul when he communicates the message of salvation. Paul is a man deeply in love with God, and his ideas and insights into the meaning of that love tumble out of him, sometimes helter-skelter in the rush to get it all said. He writes because he is anxious to share what he has been given with others; he cares for those to whom he writes, and because he cares, he wants them to be as happy as he is himself (Cf. Ph 4:4-9).

Therefore, in the letters of Paul we come in touch with the heart of a man in love. Through his heart, we peer deeply into the heart of Christ. It is through Paul that we come to Jesus; through Paul's mind that we enter into the Mind of God. As a result, divine revelation comes to us wrapped up in the moods and attitudes of Paul: the gentle, loving father (1 Tim); the stern rebuker of evil (1 Cor 5); the mystic (2 Cor 12); the suffering servant (2 Cor 4:7-5:5).

Furthermore, because Paul wrote his letters to deal with particular situations as well as out of particular frames of mind, what Paul said in anger to the Corinthians cannot be applied without qualification to all Christians everywhere. In fact, even within each letter the alert Christian is sensitive to the subtleties of Paul's thought, who was after all, a trained and careful theologian. We have to respect, therefore, the nuances of his writings. Read, for example, *1 Corinthians* and note how careful Paul is to distinguish: 1) What is from the Lord (7:10); 2) what is from himself (7:12); 3) what is custom (11:16). Much confusion will be avoided by recognizing the limitations Paul puts on his own arguments and statements.

Reading the letters of Paul and experiencing his moods, we begin to better appreciate the expression he uses so often: "The Good News is the power of God" (Rm 1:16). His writing reveals a man transformed and lifted up by the power of God, a self-righteous man with a proud past reduced to nothing so that he might be all things to all men. Yet, because of all the heady passion and faith that constitute the letters, our cold hearts and analytical minds sometimes find it difficult to grasp the truths that Paul strives so mightily to share with us. Consequently, in the long course of centuries Paul has been interpreted and misinterpreted, read and misread. By a tragic irony he has been the cause of deep division even while always upholding and setting before us the vision of the unity of the Gospel:

There is one Body, one Spirit, just as you were all called into one and the same hope when you were called. There is one Lord, one faith, one baptism, and one God who is Father of all, over all, through all and within all (Ep 4:4-6).

In spite of the difficulties a Christian should never be afraid of Paul's letters—even *Romans*! His insights into the meaning of divine revelation and his lifelong reflection on the gospel message are an unending source of growth for any individual or group who will give themselves up totally in the Spirit to an in-depth reading and sharing of Paul's letters. On the other hand, to arrive at the sublime truth and love Paul reveals, it is necessary to approach each letter—even each section of a letter—with a careful understanding of the circumstances and purpose which motivated him to write as well as an awareness of the people with whom he wished to share his spiritual gift.

The preliminary study needed to appreciate the richness of Paul's thought is well worth the effort because his ideas flow so freely and vigorously from his own faith in Jesus that it nourishes our faith as well. "Faith speaks to faith," and Paul is an exciting person who makes our growth in the Gospel exciting as well.

Gospel

The scriptural form which most vividly captures the attention of any believer in Jesus Christ is, of course, the gospel. The word "Gospel" does not primarily refer to the four gospels with which we are so familiar: *Matthew, Mark, Luke* and *John*—written expressions of the Christian message. Rather, "Gospel" means "Good News"—the total revelation of God in Christ Jesus.

Gospel is not primarily information about God, man and the universe; Gospel is fundamentally the exercise of the power of God on behalf of sinful man through the death and resurrection of God's only-begotten son, Jesus the Christ. The Gospel, in other words, is primarily a saving event—God acting in the world which was witnessed by specially chosen men, empowered in the Holy Spirit to announce what happened so that all those who accept Jesus' death and resurrection as real may enter into the eternal Kingdom of God.

However, since the original witnesses—the apostles— were not going to live forever, the Church began to write down their witness proclamation to preserve its original freshness and power for all generations. Through their written words, their apostolic presence was maintained. In the early days of the Church there were many short accounts written of Jesus, all trying to capture the truth of His saving event and its power. Yet, it is Mark to whom the Scripture scholars credit the origin of the gospel as a special literary form, as distinct from Gospel as the total revelation of the Christ event. Later, Matthew and Luke expanded and modified this form. These three gospels, along with John's gospel, came to be recognized by the believing community as divinely inspired—a true revelation from above. These four then, using the literary form of gospel, really reflect only one Gospel—Jesus Christ.

At the same time, each of the four writers has experienced the one Gospel in a unique way so that while there is a unity and harmony among the gospels there are also significant differences. The distinctive features of each are as valuable as the things they share in common. Thus, all reveal Jesus, but Mark stresses the person of Jesus as the suffering servant of Israel, the misunderstood and rejected saviour who is destined to die on the cross. John, on the other hand, emphasizes Jesus as the Word made flesh—the revelation of the Father made in power and now living in glory, but whose presence is preserved among us in the Holy Spirit. For Matthew, Jesus is the New Moses, the prophet of the New Covenant, the New Law-giver, and his Law is Love. Finally, Luke presents Jesus as a commanding figure, preordained to suffer and die, but who rose again. For Luke, nothing is left to chance; all has been foreordained by the Father.

Because of the distinctive emphasis of each gospel, they cannot all be read in the same way with the same expectations. To illustrate: a parable recorded in one gospel may have a different focus or moral than the same parable told by another gospel writer, and in order to grasp the revelation in the parable, we need to be sensitive to the gospel perspective of each author. (Try this by comparing Mt 25:14-30 with Lk 19:12-27). Thus, even though the gospels constitute one literary form, we find differences which need to be valued and responded to by Bible sharers.

Even this brief summary of the different literary forms that are used in the collection of literary masterpieces we call the Holy Bible shows that each form must be judged on its own terms. We cannot read history as if it were a parable; we cannot read a letter as if it were a poem; we cannot read a prophecy as if it were a gospel. Each form follows its own rules; each has its own value; each teaches its own kind of truth. Nevertheless, all are divine revelation.

Therefore, in reading the Scriptures we first identify the form of writing which is used to communicate the revelation, and then we arrive at its meaning. By respecting the principles that govern the form, we recognize that the very structure of the book is constitutive of what God is revealing.

The Gift of Wisdom

Does this seem like too much work? Are you discouraged by the complexity of the task? Overwhelmed? There is no need to be. God revealing Himself to sinful men and women is a rare gift, and if we devote hours of time and even years of our lives to growing in human knowledge, how much more valuable is the time spent in growing in divine wisdom. Not only have we been given this lifetime to grow in the mystery of Christ, eternity will be spent by the saints in rejoicing in the clear vision of the mystery of the Godhead. Furthermore, we do not explore the Scriptures alone and unaided. The Holy Spirit Himself is with us always, opening up meaning and urging us on.

The clearest sign that the study and sharing of the Bible is not an overwhelming task is the fact that growing numbers of Christians are doing it today. They began, as we all do, simply; but, as they understand the depths of God more fully, they are driven on by the urges of Divine Love to immerse themselves in the endless task of increasing in wisdom and grace before God and people.

The Book of Wisdom tells us of both the difficulties and the final joy that comes from learning the Mind of God and the Wisdom of Salvation:

> *"What man indeed can know the intentions of God?*
> *Who can divine the will of the Lord?*
> *The reasonings of mortals are unsure*
> *and our intentions unstable;*
> *for a perishable body presses down the soul,*
> *and this tent of clay weighs down the teeming mind.*
> *It is hard enough for us to work out what is on earth,*
> *laborious to know what lies within our reach;*
> *who, then, can discover what is in the heavens?*
> *As for your intention, who could have learnt it, had*
> *you not granted Wisdom*
> *and sent your Holy Spirit from above?*
> *Thus have the paths of those on earth been*
> *straightened*
> *and men been taught what pleases you,*
> *and saved, by Wisdom"* (Wi 9:13-18).

CHAPTER SIX

GOD STILL INTERVENES TODAY

The earliest books of the Bible, like *Genesis* and *Exodus*, reflect the Hebrew nation's search for its roots—its origins as God's chosen people. Later books, especially the books of the prophets, were God's revelation to His already-formed people who were drifting away from their commitment to Him (called Covenant) and turning to false gods and false values. Israel was backsliding, and the prophets were sent by the Lord God to correct His people and bring them back to renewed dedication to God and perfect obedience of His Law. The books of prophets, therefore, are masterpieces of threat and promise.

Subsequent books, such as *Proverbs, Job* and the rest of the wisdom literature, sought to plumb the mystery of good and evil, a perennial question of daily human existence. These beautiful and sensitive masterpieces were written by men who were living in a rather stable believing community and had the leisure to reflect on the unanswered questions of their religion. Why, they asked, do the innocent suffer? Is there life after death? Why were we born? Well aware of the importance of the nation, the tribe and the community, they now began to ask: Where does the individual fit into all this? How important is he? Does his life count?

Yet as important as each of these forty-six books of the Old Testament was in itself, together they had an even greater importance in terms of Christian faith. Together they prepared the chosen people of God for the coming of the promised Messiah, Jesus Christ. He was to save them from their sins and deliver them from the bondage of the Law so that they might live a new and eternal life of joy and peace.

The Mystery of Jesus

As part of His eternal plan, God set aside a special people to be in harmony with Him so that He might manifest to them and through them the depth of His love for all mankind by means of the death, resurrection and glorification of Jesus. The resurrection of Jesus, therefore, marks a turning point not only in the history of the Jewish people, but also in the history of the whole world. What started out as a religion for a people became the salvation for all. This striking event was an active intervention by God into the affairs of men. It was a wonderful and decisive overcoming of the power of evil, opening up to those who believe a new world of holiness, freedom and light. All twenty-seven books of the New Testament are the fulfillment of the teaching of the Old because they reveal the meaning of the life and teaching of Jesus Christ.

Just after his resurrection, Jesus appeared to two of his disciples on the road to Emmaus, and he explained to them how the Old Testament revealed the significance of his life. He said to them:

> *"Was it not ordained that the Christ should suffer and so enter into his glory?" Then, starting with Moses and going through all the prophets, he explained to them the passages throughout the scriptures that were about himself* (Lk 24:26).

So earth-shaking was the Jesus event that it formed a new people, rooted in the life of Judea but drawing new life from the presence of the Holy Spirit sent from Jesus to be with them always as their guide, their advocate and their comfort. As time went on, the differences between the Jews who refused to accept Jesus and the Jews and Gentiles who did accept him became more and more marked. It was inevitable that eventually the Jews would respond to the new Presence in their midst by severe persecution and ultimate expulsion of the Christians—or Followers of the Way, as they were called—from the synagogues and temple worship. It was this opposition of the Jews that compelled the Christians to establish their own customs and liturgical practices which slowly, but dramatically, divorced them from the regular life of Jewish worship.

For the newly evolving Christian community, the link to Jesus was always the apostolic witness. The apostles had been especially chosen by Jesus himself to live with him and to accompany him on his preaching missions in order that they might bear witness to his person, his teaching and his wonderful works. After his ascension into heaven, the apostles went about preaching and healing as Jesus had done, proclaiming the Good News that Jesus had risen from the dead and would give salvation to those who believed in him. As a result of their ministry, they gathered believers around themselves and established what has become the Church Universal, whose organization and structure evolved, as do all societies, to meet the exigencies of the New Times. Nevertheless, in all this development, it has always been the apostles to whom the Church has looked as the final agents of revelation.

Events not Philosophy

Christianity has become for many people merely a philosophy of life, an ideal for human living. Perhaps it is the way we are educated in this country, but we seem to be more attuned to general ideas than specific facts; we are readily able to assent to abstractions, even though we have not given much consideration to their consequences. Because of this approach to life, we are more at home with and responsive to the ideals of Christianity than to the facts of revelation. Yet, that is the way divine revelation comes to us—through unique events and specific facts.

The Bible is concerned with the positive, direct and constant intervention of Divine Love into the ordinary affairs of men; the interventions, however, always take place with perfect respect and due regard for man's independence and freedom. In revealing Himself, God does not destroy the autonomy which He has given to natural beings. While transcending the laws of nature, God never violates them; rather, God always acts with man and in man in terms of man's complete reasonable, rational, free humanness. He shapes man to live in His presence through love. He draws man to Himself through the circumstances into which he was born and in which he lives; He molds man through the inbred talents He has given him, the disposition of his heart and his habit of mind. He climaxes it all through the wonderful revelation of His love found in the Scriptures, and the experience of His power exercised constantly in the Holy Spirit.

Christian life does not fly in the face of reason or contravene the accepted, obvious and normal laws of nature. If the laws of nature were constantly violated by God, nature itself would cease to have purpose and meaning. If God were always to impede man's freedom in the conduct of his own affairs, God would be denying the goodness of His own creation. In other words, the Scriptures do not give us a magical view of the world and life in it.

Nevertheless, Sacred Scripture does teach that God communicates the extent of His love for man through marvelous manifestations of His power, although only the man of faith can perceive them. Ordinary events become extraordinary because the believer is empowered by the Holy Spirit to see the deeper reality and acknowledge it as the manifestation of God's mercy.

The books of the Old Testament, for instance, do not just tell what happened to the Israelites; they tell us why they happened. In the *Book of Jeremiah* we do not have simply a recounting of how Judah fell to the Babylonians, rather Jeremiah reveals the reason for its fall—it was a punishment from God because the Israelites refused to free their slaves (Cf. Jr 34:8-22). Again, the *Second Book of Kings* explains that the fall of the Northern Kingdom and the deportation of its people was not just the result of a human act of war:

This happened because they had not obeyed the voice of Yahweh their God and had broken his covenant, violating all that Moses the servant of Yahweh had laid down. They neither listened to it nor put it into practice (2 K 18:12).

Miracles

Jesus worked wonders. The Christian cannot believe in the Jesus presented to us in the gospels without accepting the fact that he worked marvelous signs that amazed the crowds and put the people in awe. Jesus' mighty deeds and his teaching about the coming of the kingdom of God are inextricably linked together. This is especially true of the resurrection on which, as St. Paul tells us, all else stands or falls (1 Cor 15:14). At the same time, the way some of the wonders are reported by the believing gospel writer makes it difficult for the modern reader to know exactly "what happened."

Much biblical discussion is taking place today on the historicity of miracles, and there are two extreme ways of looking at them. On the one hand, some say that every miracle of Jesus, or even every miracle in the Old Testament, happened exactly the way it is written, with every last detail accurately recorded for a believing posterity. On the other hand, some go to the opposite extreme and say that no miracles ever took place, but rather that unusual circumstances were twisted into miracles even though natural events alone could account for what had happened. However, because believers see God everywhere, they argue, they see His special power even in natural events. This approach to miracles is called *demythologizing.*

For example, when, according to Matthew, Jesus cast the devils out of the two Gadarene demoniacs and sent them into the large herd of pigs that drowned themselves in the sea (Mt 8:28-34), must this account be accepted as true exactly as it is written? If so, how do you account for the fact that Luke (8:26-39) has only one demoniac, and his story has a different point? Or, is this incident only a figurative, but vivid, way the gospel writers have to describe the effect Jesus had on people?

The gospel miracles are a stimulating problem because, when we come to grips with it and seek to solve it in faith, it opens up whole new dimensions of scriptural meaning for us. Miracles are not a problem to be feared, therefore, but explored. In fact, we should never be afraid to reflect on the reality of Christ's miracles because in exploring their significance we come to a more profound understanding of the mystery of Christ and the revelation of God's love.

While there are many commentaries which treat of miracles, the whole matter can get too complicated for the ordinary Bible sharer and become more disturbing than helpful in growing in the mystery of Jesus Christ. To avoid that, without being overly-simplistic, the following criteria can be used profitably to evaluate each particular miracle in the New Testament in a way which enables us to arrive at the truth the writer is trying to reveal.

Criteria for Evaluating Miracles

1. If you question the historicity of a particular miracle, you must have a reason for doing so, since the presumption is that it did occur. You cannot begin by assuming that no miracles ever took place. On the other hand, if a miracle seems a little far-fetched (Jesus causing a fig tree to wither like magic—Mt 21:19), it would be reasonable to ask why the author attributed this deed to him. (In the case of the fig tree, commentators think it was a literary device to highlight the sterility of the Jews in their rejections of Jesus—a parable in action, as it were).

2. If you reject a miracle, you must question what else is necessarily rejected. To illustrate: If you deny that Jesus cast out real devils, are you also denying the reality of devils? What are the consequences of this denial? If the consequences are

opposed to the orthodox faith, obviously the miraculous nature of the event must be preserved.

3. Is what is being rejected related to faith? If so, how intimate is that relationship? (In our example, can we believe in Jesus, even if we do not accept the reality of devils? If not, the devils must be real; if we can still believe in Jesus with believing in devils, they *may not* be real).

4. How does the ordinary teaching of the Church, to say nothing of the extraordinary, guide us in the matter? (Does Christian tradition generally teach that there are real devils and Jesus effectively exorcised them? Or, does the common faith of Christians admit the possibility of another explanation for what Jesus did? I, frankly, opt for devils, but there is an opinion to the contrary).

5. Finally, it is essential always to bear in mind that we cannot choose between a Jesus of history who never worked wonders and a Christ of faith who did them constantly. If there was a Jesus at all—and there certainly was and is—he inaugurated the Kingdom of God in this world both in words and signs. Jesus preached an eschatological message, and the gospels present his miracles as signs that the Kingdom of God had arrived.

Jesus said: "The works I do in my Father's name are my witness" (Jn 10:25).

The Bible as Guide for Today

For all their importance, ultimately the Bible was not written just to record past interventions of God into the affairs of men; it only uses them to bring us to the point where we can see, in faith, how God is acting in our lives today. The Bible is a guide, revealing how we can live in God's kingdom, rejoice in His presence, be transformed by His power and love with His love. The Scriptures are the revelation given to us, members of God's chosen people, in order that we might be happy even in this vale of tears. The source of our happiness is the profound realization that in Jesus Christ we were created out of love to live in love, and to be with God for all eternity. In Jesus, holiness and happiness become identical, since it is impossible for the truly holy man not to be happy and the truly happy man not to be holy.

This understanding of the intimate union between living in God's presence and the reality of happiness solves a problem which many Christians seem to have: they look upon moral goodness as a way of purchasing God's favor, instead of seeing it as the effect of God's love. When we have God's favor, we experience His love in our lives and, therefore are transformed by His presence so that we become His children—capable of being good and doing good—capable of loving as Christ loves. It is precisely in the doing of good through love that we achieve happiness both here and hereafter, since we cannot be truly happy without being truly loving. St. John puts it this way:

> *If anyone acknowledges that Jesus is the Son of God, God lives in him, and he in God. We ourselves have known and put our faith in God's love towards ourselves. God is love and anyone who lives in love lives in God, and God lives in him* (1 Jn 4:15-16).

Christian happiness, of course, is not the fleeting satisfaction that comes from the senses or immediate personal gain. Rather, it is the deep and abiding happiness that comes from the awareness of being a child of God and member of Christ's body: knowing who we are, where we are going, why we exist. Christian happiness is knowing the answers to the basic transcendental questions human beings have been asking from the beginning of time. It is the truth that makes us free. (Jn 8:32).

The Sacred Scriptures are, therefore, a true guide to life, but not as a book of directions containing rules to be followed and laws to be obeyed. They are the revelation of how we can grow in happiness by recognizing God's loving hand in each and every action of our lives, guiding, directing, shaping, raising us up and bringing us into ever more intimate union with Himself. The insignificant becomes significant because

God is acting. When the Samaritan woman went to the well for her usual daily water supply, that insignificant act which she had done so often became a momentous occasion. There Jesus spoke to her and gave her living water.

Through the Scriptures God speaks to us, and when we hear His voice, we are filled with awe and can only say with St. Paul: "Oh the depths of the riches and the wisdom and the knowledge of God" (Rm 11:33).

CHAPTER SEVEN

THE TOTAL MEANING OF THE BIBLE

As a result of our analysis of the complex elements which are constitutive of the Holy Bible as it has been handed down to us in the Church of Christ, we might really begin to doubt we can ever know what it says. So we are faced with a challenging question when all is said and done: Can anybody read the Bible and really arrive at its meaning?

The Problem of Meaning

There are two answers to the question. The one extreme says: Yes, anyone can read it, if you have faith. It was written for ordinary people and all you have to do is pick it up and let the Lord speak to you.

As we said earlier, this simplistic understanding can degenerate into magic. Readers who think this way expect God to solve their problems and cast His light on their personal spiritual dilemmas "on demand." They "cut" the Bible to force the Lord to speak right now, on their terms.

Another manifestation of this kind of approach to the Bible occurs when readers think that every word can be understood according to its common use in English today. Differences in cultures, times, world views and the like are overlooked or ignored. New translations disturb such readers, since differences in translation reveal the complexity of the original writing.

The other extreme says: very special skills are required to read the Bible—a background in biblical history, theology, geography, culture, language, etc. Don't read the Bible without expert guidance. This is particularly important, so the argument runs, for Catholics so they do not fall into "private" interpretations that will lead them away from their faith.

The truth lies in-between the two extremes. The Holy Bible is not the newspaper; it was not written in modern English and certainly reflects a culture (or more exactly, cultures) and world views vastly different from our own. Therefore, in order to arrive at the meaning of what God wishes to reveal to us that has relevancy for our own day requires prayer, hard work, perseverance, and the willingness to live with mystery, even while attempting to plumb its depths. For the Bible is not a single book; as we have seen, it is a collection of many individual books, some of which are themselves collections of other literary products or even collections of speeches made by men and women who have spoken with God and heard His word in their hearts.

At the same time, it is not too complicated. Believers with an ordinary education plus a willingness to use biblical guides can grasp the meaning in a way which brings rich spiritual fruit to themselves, their families, their friends and the Church.

Fundamental to our approaching the Scriptures is our Christian belief that Almighty God is the Author of the whole Bible. That is, He inspired human writers so that what they wrote reflects His own Divine Mind to such an extent that the Sacred Scriptures truly are the word of God. Just how His inspiration works, however, has been a matter of debate over the ages, as human beings have tried to come to grips with this intervention of the Divine into the intellectual life of men and women.

Total Meaning

With all we have said up to now as a background, there are two stages in arriving at the total meaning of the Bible as the living word of God and revelation of divine mystery:

1) Determine what the biblical text says of itself (called "exegeting the text"); 2) Determine what the biblical text says to us today (called the "hermeneutic of the text"). We cannot arrive at stage two, however, without first having some notion of stage one, the literal meaning of the biblical text. It is in the literal meaning that we find the fundamental revelation of God, even for us in our day. All subsequent use or understanding of biblical writing depends upon and must be in harmony with the first and most basic sense of Scripture—the literal sense.

Literary Form

The first step in arriving at the literal meaning is to determine the form of expression the author selected to use— called by scripture scholars, the literary form. Thus, a writer may express himself through a poem or a story or a letter or a gospel. In each case, God has used—inspired—the literary ingenuity of man to reveal some aspect of His truth.

In order, however, to fully appreciate the significance of the literary form the modern reader needs to grasp something of the purpose of the book, its historical origins, and the times in which it was written. Fortunately, many books and articles are available to assist us in this task.

Without due respect for the literal meaning, we can find ourselves embroiled in emotional arguments over "historicity." Understanding the literal sense of Scripture provides balance.

Stage Two

Yet, no matter how important it is for today's reader of Scripture to understand the literal meaning of the text, to mature in faith we go further. We strive to discern the significance of the Bible for our lives today as well.

The gospels, for example, were not written as mere

histories of Jesus' life; far more, they are the preaching and teaching of the apostles handed on to us which enable us to put our trust in Jesus in even these sophisticated times. At the Last Supper Jesus prayed personally for us who hear the words of his apostles when he said to his Heavenly Father: "I pray not only for these (the apostles) but for those also who through their words will believe in me" (Jn 17:20).

The total meaning of the Scriptures, therefore, is grasped by us today only when we hear the words of the apostles in Christ's Church and put our faith in Jesus.

The Holy Spirit

We can read the Scriptures which were written in the past and get meaning from them for our present because they were written through the Holy Spirit. The Holy Spirit is the living link between the human author and the human reader. It is the Spirit who enables us to put on the mind of Christ today (cf. Cor 2:10-16).

When the Holy Spirit inspired the human author, He moved the human writer to use all his personal talents and ingenuity to create a work of literature that would express the mind of God. The Spirit moved him to find the right images, select the right theme, recall the significant events, achieve the proper effect (cf. Jn 16:7-15). As a result, the work that the writer created is truly the word of God, having a life of its own, like the seed, now independent of the writer, but nevertheless the product of his creative understanding of God.

So, too, when the Holy Spirit leads us to read the Scriptures, He empowers us to see not just what happened in the past, but what is happening now.

In the first chapter of the *Acts of the Apostles*, Jesus tells his disciples: "You will receive power when the Holy Spirit comes on you, and then you will be my witnesses not only in Jerusalem, but throughout Judea and Samaria, and indeed to the ends of the earth" (Ac 1:8). And then the entire *Book of Acts* is the unfolding of how that power to witness was actualized in the early Church and how, through faith, the word of God spread throughout the world.

Power Today

Furthermore, that power to witness still operates in believers today. We are the Church now as the early Christians were the Church then. The Spirit transcends time and space, and the word that reveals His power in the early Church also reveals His power in the modern Church. Now, as then, He gives His gifts so that each age is the Church of *Acts.*

When Paul wrote to the Corinthians revealing the nature of Christian love, he was writing for us as well. Love gave the Corinthians the power to be patient, kind, gentle and hopeful; and it gives us the same power.

Again, so many of the experiences that are given expression in the Scriptures are ones with which we are personally familiar. There are few Christians, exhausted by the exhortations of friends and pastors, who have not cried to heaven with Job 7:17-21. And most of us still have enough of the unredeemed in us to appreciate fully what Paul means in *Romans* 7:14-24.

Questions For Today

A final example of arriving at the meaning of Scriptures for us today: Read *Ephesians* 1:3-14, and then prayerfully consider these questions: 1) What does it mean to be "chosen?" 2) What is the "freedom" the passage speaks about? Do you experience that? How? 3) Does your practice of religion bring you a sense of release and freedom? or inadequacy and guilt? 4) How have you experienced "the pledge of the Spirit?" 5) Do you think that is too much to demand of religion?

There are no black and white answers to questions of this kind. Indeed, in reading the Scriptures and coming to grips with the mysteries they reveal, we very often find that we have more questions than answers, but they are questions that stimulate faith and lead us to turn with renewed confidence to Jesus who is the "way, the truth and the life."

CHAPTER EIGHT

FORMING BIBLE SHARING GROUPS

From all that has been said so far, it might seem that studying the Bible and deriving meaning for life from it is too complicated for the modern, busy American. It is not! It is not because, first and foremost, God's word itself is powerful and written for simple men and women who hunger to know His love. Knowing and loving His children, God wrote the right book for them to read, savor and share; He knew their limits and their abilities, and respecting both, He wrote the Bible. Furthermore, we are especially blessed today because there are so many resources available to us to make reading the Bible enjoyable, even though it may also be challenging. Given the educational level we enjoy in this country, there is nothing more exciting which we Christians can do with our minds than to grow in the knowledge of God's own word, the revelation of the mystery of Christ.

To repeat what was said at the beginning, only three things are really necessary: a good Bible, believing people, and the Holy Spirit. We are now ready to discuss the process of Bible sharing itself, in which all three come together to lead us to a deeper appreciation of the meaning of the word of God for our lives.

Private Bible study can be a pretty lonely occupation; it may be personally very satisfying, of course, and we all need to devote time to private study of the word. In this way we can understand it ourselves and try to teach and evangelize others. Still, when we only study the Bible we can be just filling ourselves up with a lot of head knowledge that we may or or may not be able to translate into experience of faith. Bible sharing, on the other hand, is a way to build on our personal study of the Bible to grow in Jesus.

Loving Exchange

As we have seen Bible sharing is a form of group discussion. It is based on the principle that the dynamics of interpersonal relationships will lead the group to a new and more complete understanding of the matter under discussion. In other words, if you put together a group of people with fresh and carefully thought-out ideas and give them a chance to talk to each other about their common interest, their exchange will bring each member of the group to a new awareness of the subject.

Therefore, those who are invited to participate in a Bible sharing group should be Christians who can give themselves freely to this principle of group discussion in order to come to draw Jesus more intimately. They should be willing both to explain their own insights into the meaning of Scripture to others and to listen respectfully to the insights which the others offer to them. If this is the underlying attitude, then the discussion process itself will lead to deeper understanding by the group as a whole which each member can then appropriate for his own. The result of this kind of exchange is a tremendous experience of personal growth in the Lord Jesus.

This exchange of ideas forces each to find the best way to express what he wants to say and, at the same time, the questioning and probing of others enables him to reexamine his ideas to see if they really are as insightful as he had thought. Over a period of time, the discipline of exchange will enable each person to ask the right questions at the very beginning of his private study period; he will know what he is looking for and can enter into a more fruitful dialogue with the human author of the word of God who is leading us to Jesus. This point becomes clearer when we see the kind of questions which the group discusses in order to get at the meaning of Scripture passages.

Perceptible Growth

All the methods and procedures of Bible sharing are no more than efforts to provide each individual member with an experience of growth each time he participates in a group session, so that he feels that it is worth the sacrifice of time and energy it requires to exchange insight. It only takes one or two sessions for someone who feels that he is not getting much out of the session to give up; it might start out as a postponement, or a feeling that he can afford to miss one session, but it will not be long before he has quietly dropped out of the group. Good will is not enough; it takes growth, and for Christians that means growth in Jesus as Lord.

Therefore, we are going to explore what practices of the group encourage personal growth and give the satisfied feeling of having done something valuable, and what impede that experience. For example, if someone gets involved in a Bible sharing group in which one of the members insists on being the teacher for the whole group, he will probably drop out, since no one likes to be talked down to or have someone else force his opinion on him. If anyone wants to have a teacher, there are plenty to whom he can willingly go. In Bible sharing all come together as equals, and no individual should try to dominate, either through ramming his ideas down people's throats or giving endless witness without listening to what God is doing in others' lives as well.

Guidelines for Growth

Here, then, are a few simple guidelines that can help each group experience that welcome growth:

1. *Have the right number of participants for free discussion.*

The ideal group size for Bible sharing is 10 to 12 people; 8 to 14 people are outside limits. Fewer than eight members makes it difficult to get enough creative ideas and insights for stimulating discussion. If there are more than fourteen people, not everyone will be able to participate freely, and those who do not get the opportunity to contribute will begin to feel excluded and more than likely will eventually drop out.

To insure that ten to twelve people will actually attend each session, it is a good idea to have a pool of at least twenty people to draw on. Given the demands of jobs, families, and the unexpected conflicts of schedules, not everyone will be able to come to every session, so there should be a basic group that is large enough to compensate for the unavoidable absenteeism.

2. *Prepare!*

Those who attend the session cannot come just to listen and absorb; for fruitful group sharing, they must come filled with something to give as well as to receive. No observers, please. Unless each participant has studied the passages to be discussed ahead of time and has arrived at some clear idea of their meaning, the discussion will not be an exchange of insights and no growth will occur. When sharing something as profound and rich as the word of God, in-depth, personal preparation through study, prayer, meditation and reflection must have preceded it.

3. *Stick to the Bible.*

The people who take part in Bible sharing have to be willing to stick to the Bible. It is very frustrating for someone to come to a sharing session expecting to discuss the Bible to discover when they get there that they are going to have to listen to talk about children, jobs, the economy or politics. Sometimes because of the pressing problems people have, they begin to share these instead of the Bible which gets pushed into the background. Bible sharing has only one purpose: to share insights into the meaning of the Sacred Scriptures for our lives today. When each session is finished, the participants should have a deeper understanding and appreciation of the text they have been working on together in the Holy Spirit.

4. *Shop around.*

Bible sharing, because it is such an intensely personal experience, can take place only in an atmosphere of mutual respect, trust and love; it flourishes best when the members of the group are compatible in outlook, interests (in the Bible) and taste. Styles differ, and not all styles appeal to all of us. Therefore, if someone feels uncomfortable in one group he should shop around until he finds the group which is most compatible with his own view of life and personality. There is nothing sacrosanct about the make-up of a group. Each should find the group which helps him to grow most in the Lord.

This does not mean that all members have to have the same education, backgrounds or incomes. As a matter of fact, a diversity of gifts, including age, sex and ecclesial traditions, contributes to fruitful sharing. Love is the bond that opens up each member of the group to God's gifts in the others.

5. *Reach out for new members.*

While the word of a good Bible sharing group eventually gets around and begins to attract people to it, each group should actively seek out new members to bring into the sharing experience. Unless the effort is made to expand, there is a danger that the group will become closed in on itself; its habits of mind, discussion and outlook will become too fixed for real growth. Any group of people needs the challenge of new ideas and new faces, so that the dynamic groups will be those that welcome new members and have regular programs for incorporating them into the discussion process and group fellowship.

This might mean that one or two group members will

spend extra time with the newcomers to help them get off to a good start in Bible sharing. The welcoming team should show them how to study the Bible in preparation for sharing: how to use introductions, footnotes, cross-references. It should acquaint them with the resource materials available to the group and initiate them into the unique customs each group has for fruitful participation.

Of course, when the group gets too big, it will become necessary for it to divide and that is the surest sign of God's blessing. Our Lord sent his disciples out two-by-two; today, we are the Lord's disciples, and when a group gets above 14 active, sharing members it should divide and form new groups to spread the Good News of the Kingdom.

6. *Bring in the young.*

Whenever Christian young people are old enough to have questions about the meaning of life and sufficient insight to be able to handle adult ideas, they should be encouraged to become members of adult Bible sharing groups. The norm for admittance is not chronological age but intellectual, emotional and spiritual maturity which results in the desire to grow in the Lord. Many believing teen-agers are far more likely to really grow in faith by sharing God's word with adults than with their peers. There is sufficient evidence to conclude that sixteen-year-olds talking about God in a classroom will not mature as quickly or perceptively as they will if they have the opportunity to share their experiences in faith with a broad spectrum of adult believers who are sincerely concerned about the Lord. Given parental influence, children sharing the word with their parents would be ideal, but if for some reason (lack of good communication, for example) that is impossible, perhaps they can share with their parents' friends. Furthermore, young people not only learn from adults, they can also contribute much to the adults' growth in the word of God.

At the same time, as a result of being members of an adult group, they may be inspired to become leaders of Bible sharing groups among their less mature peers. There are instances where young people were so excited by their experience of sharing the Bible with adults that they developed an apostolate among their younger friends and peers, leading them as well as themselves into a rich Gospel experience.

7. *Have a good mix.*

A Bible sharing group is enriched when its members come from varying backgrounds: men and women, young and old, married and single, rich and poor, well-educated and less-educated. All meet on common ground when they gather around the word of God with the desire to grow in the experience of His love. Hence, there should be no reluctance to actively work for a wide variety of people in each group; variety keeps insights fresh as divergent backgrounds provide different ways of interpreting the word of God.

Nevertheless, there are certain classes of people who are immediate candidates for Bible sharing. First, of course, are the lectors of the parish. No one should be permitted to proclaim the Scriptures in the public, official worship of the Church for whom the Bible has not become a deeply personal document. The lector does not just read words written on a page; he bears witness to his own faith experience of the truth of revelation and his own understanding of the word of God which is rooted in his heart and is given expression daily in the manner of his life. It is impeding the communication of the word of God in our churches when lectors get up in front of their Christian communities these days and try to read a passage of Scripture that they have not thoroughly digested and made their own in faith. There is far more to reading in the liturgy than being able to find the place in the lectionary and knowing how to pronounce some of those Hebrew names. The lector is commissioned to proclaim faith—from faith to beget faith—so he needs to appreciate the meaning of divine revelation as he has personally experienced it in his own life.

Religion teachers, both in parochial schools and CCD, are obvious candidates for membership in Bible sharing groups. Since personal growth in the word of God is a lifelong process, we never get too old or too smart not to need to share the word with our fellow Christians. Sometimes teachers get "professional" in their efforts to spread the Kingdom among the young, but the communication of salvation transcends "professionalism." Like dying, proclaiming the Gospel cannot be done "professionally." Bible sharing keeps the professionals on the track of honest and realistic growth in the Lord.

Members of the parish council and those engaged in social ministry for the parish should also regularly participate in Bible sharing because they all play leading parts in the life of the Church. What they do, what they say, the decisions they make, the actions they undertake, the programs they inaugurate, all of these have profound effect on the way Jesus Christ is proclaimed as Saviour and Lord by the total life of the parish community. For example, it is impossible to carry on an active faith-filled social ministry unless it is personally and not just institutionally rooted in the word of God; without the constant personal reading and sharing of Scripture, we can become simply institutional social activists instead of personal Gospel witnesses. The Holy Bible, shared in faith, on the other hand, gives us steady guidance and support in all our ministries. As Paul wrote to Timothy: "Through the reading of Scripture the man who is dedicated to God becomes fully equipped and ready for any good work" (2 Tm 3:17).

With the many demands that are made of priests today, it is unreasonable to expect that your parish priest would be able to attend every Bible sharing session. He should always be welcome, of course, but he cannot really be depended upon for continual guidance. One of the many advantages of Bible sharing is that a priest's presence is not necessary for fruitful sharing even though it may be helpful and welcome from time to time.

8. *Encourage fellowship and mutual support.*

Bible sharing is only the start of many wonderful things the Lord wants to work in our lives. People who share the word of God with one another soon discover that the intellectual understanding that results and the sense of genuine concern that comes from hearing personal witness generates a spirit of Christian love and fellowship among the members. What starts out as a discussion group soon reveals itself as a small Christian community whose members actively support and encourage one another in their moments of physical, emotional and psychological need. They can do this because they are growing in the experience of the power of God.

Not only do members of a group support one another, groups as a whole find themselves entering into fellowship with other groups through Eucharistic celebrations, periodic joint meetings during which they hear good biblical preachers, regional Word of God Days, and social gatherings. While individuals in the groups lose the sense of frustration that comes from trying to live a Christian life alone in a pagan environment, the groups soon begin to see themselves united to other groups all over the country and the world. The sense of isolation lifted, Christians, both lay and clergy, find they want to work with one another in developing programs of outreach to bring everyone into union with the Lord. As a result of mutual encouragement, Bible sharing groups and their members are in the vanguard of the evangelizing efforts of the Church.

9. *Meet on a regular basis.*

Once it is formed, a Bible sharing group should meet on a regular basis no less than once every two weeks, including summers. If it meets less frequently, there is bound to be a lack of continuity without which there will not be an experience of personal growth. Ideally, a Bible sharing group should meet once a week, at the same time, for one and a half hours, since it takes about that amount of time to develop a discussion of any depth. Each session has to have enough time for prayer, silence, simple reflection, and song, as well as an introduction to the passage being shared and the discussion itself. Less time makes things rushed and an exchange of significant and deeply personal insights cannot usually be achieved.

On the other hand, most of us do not have the capacity to concentrate with the energy Bible sharing requires for more than two hours at a stretch. Although some may be able to do it a few times, if the sessions drag on too often, those members of the group that find the protracted session too much of an inconvenience will begin to drop out, and as they drop out the group will become smaller until it is too small to support Bible sharing.

Each group should have a regular means of communication among its members to remind them of the time and place of the meeting, particularly if the meeting place rotates among members' homes. It also gives the members the opportunity to inform the group if they will be absent. It is important that all meetings always start and stop on time.

10. *Start easy.*

In announcing the start of a Bible sharing group, it might be worthwhile to advertise that the group will meet for just ten sessions or so and then reevaluate whether it wants to continue to meet. Sometimes we are reluctant to commit ourselves to something which is without end, whereas we are willing to try something new for a specific period of time. Actually, after ten weeks, most groups willingly go beyond to become ongoing Bible sharing groups.

11. *Meet in a place that is free of distractions.*

The meeting place should be easily accessible by all, comfortable and informal. It should not be drafty or stuffy, neither too hot nor too cold; it should be adequately lighted and free of noise and distracting interruptions: telephones, door bells, radios, televisions, young children. Some groups meet in homes, while others prefer to meet in classrooms or public areas. Seating should be arranged in a way which allows all the members to be able to look at one another directly and to talk easily and quietly.

While refreshments are certainly an appropriate part of

Christian fellowship, they should be given out before or after the discussion, but not in the middle. There is no need to take a break after only an hour of talk, and balancing cups and saucers and passing around cream and sugar seriously breaks the flow of conversation and the exchange of insights. In other words, once the discussion starts, each participant should be free to give their total attention to the sharing of the word of God.

12. *Be flexible.*

It is clear from all that we have been saying that there is no single ideal structure for a Bible sharing group; there is not one method of sharing which works equally well for all. Rather, Bible sharing is a loose form of discussion which will vary considerably from group to group depending on the people who form the group. The easiest principle a group can follow—and the best—is *Be flexible* and respond, in the Spirit, to the needs of the members as they arise.

CHAPTER NINE

GUIDELINES FOR CONDUCTING MEETINGS

The key to fruitful, stimulating and enjoyable Bible sharing is open, free and substantial interchange of ideas and personal witness relevant to particular texts of the Holy Bible. Each group will arrive at its own procedures which are best able to meet its needs as a group as well as to respect the needs of each of its members. With these two basic principles in mind, this chapter explains some general guidelines that can contribute to the effectiveness of any Bible sharing experience.

The Bible Sharing Leader

The Bible sharing leader is the facilitator of discussion; it is this person's function to ease and promote the exchange of insights into and experiences of the word of God among the members of the group. The leadership can rotate from session to session; in fact, it is a good idea if it does, so that no one person becomes to be regarded as the "teacher" at whose feet all the others sit. Bible sharing is not just Bible study because in sharing all participants are equal in both giving and receiving. The teacher has an important part to play in Bible study; but Bible sharing is not the place for the teacher to preside.

On the other hand, if there is one person to whom God has given special leadership ability and who is particularly adept in stimulating discussion and promoting the common welfare of the group, that person might function as leader for an extended period of time. However, whether the leadership rotates weekly, monthly, or whether it remains permanently with one person, leadership is only one part of a total cooperative effort by all members to promote the greatest possible exchange of ideas and insights through the extensive participation of all. Each member, therefore, should actively assist the leader in inviting participation, sharing time and avoiding domination by one or two.

The leader should contact members to ascertain who will be present or absent, and he should oversee the physical arrangements so that all members are comfortable and the group will be free of distractions and interruptions.

It is the leader's responsibility to set the limits of the passage to be discussed and plan the general thrust of the sharing session. To do this, he should select the passage to be shared (it will grow organically out of the preceding session, of course) and prepare a brief introduction to it to be given to the group. For this purpose, he will have to do some special study so that he can give the background on the passage: author, purpose, time of composition, the place of the present passage in the total composition, and literary form.

Stimulating Questions

The basic and primary task of the leader is to provide a series of open-ended questions which will stimulate the group's discussion of the sacred text. In the next chapter we will give some examples of different kinds of questions that can be formulated to invite discussion. In general, they are questions which cannot be answered by yes or no or some fact, but rather they demand reasoning and explanation. For example, one would not ask, in the discussion of *Ephesians* 1:3-14, Did God choose you? But a good question to stimulate an exchange of insights and experiences might be: What does it mean to be chosen? Or, How have you experienced being chosen in your life?

The Holy Spirit

An atmosphere of prayer is essential for fruitful sharing of the Holy Bible. The sacred writers could not have written down God's revelation except for the inspiration of the Holy Spirit; in the same way, we cannot expect to understand divine revelation except under the guidance of the Holy Spirit. The Bible is His book and reveals His meaning, and Jesus sent the Spirit to us in order to lead us to complete truth (Jn 16:13).

Prayer styles vary extensively from group to group, and no one way of prayer is to be preferred over another. The group itself must decide what manner of prayer it feels most at home with and which seems to bear the richest fruit in terms of Bible sharing. Nevertheless, three elements should be present in the total prayer experience of the group:

1. The prayer should be biblical; that is, it should flow out of and lead back to the Scriptures that are being shared.

2. It should be both structured and free. There are certain things a group should be praying for in each session, and the leader should see to it that these needs of the group are articulated—not, obviously, for God's sake, but for the sake of the group. At the same time, prayer should not be cast in a rigid and repetitive mode. Perhaps a group will always want to include the Our Father or Hail Mary as part of its prayer, still it should not be limited to just "formalized prayer."

3. It should be participative. Each member of the group should, at some point, have the opportunity to voice aloud his own inner pleadings of the Spirit—whether it be to praise or to petition. Such spontaneous prayer will usually flow out of the texts that have been discussed and the meaning of which has been shared.

A popular form of devotion is to "pray the Scriptures" in which personal prayer is encouraged to flow organically out of the reading of Scripture. In this devotion, the Scriptures are not read so much to nourish the mind as to inspire prayer which is direct, immediate communication with God. It is a marvelously joyful method of approaching prayer.

In Bible sharing, however, prayer is not so much the focus

of the session as is growth in faith through a deepened appreciation of the word of God. "Praying the Scriptures" will be enhanced by substantial Bible sharing, but prayer does not, cannot, replace the sharing of the word itself. Still, there cannot be fruitful Bible sharing without heartfelt prayer in the Holy Spirit. "Since the Spirit is our life, let us be directed by the Spirit" (Gal 5:25).

CHAPTER TEN

MODELS FOR BIBLE SHARING

Once the group of Spirit-filled people who are anxious to grow in their appreciation of the word of God has been formed, there are a number of ways of conducting its sessions. This chapter describes some of these ways which many have tried and found to be fruitful. Since Bible sharing is characterized by flexibility, everything that is said here will not be suitable for every group; yet, some of the ideas will be helpful when incorporated into the group's own method of sharing.

The Opening Prayer

After the ten to fourteen members have gathered in a convenient and comfortable spot free of distractions and have settled down for serious sharing, the leader should begin with a prayer. It is better if it is a prayer which, in some way, focuses on the Scripture that will be shared. It need not be long, but should reflect the attitudes of those gathered, and while praising God, it should also ask His blessings on those who are about to explore the mysteries that He is revealing.

The Introduction

After the opening prayer is concluded, the leader should give a brief introduction to the scriptural passage which will form the basis for sharing. He should identify it, describe the place it holds in revelation, and give its literary form; he should identify the author, the purpose and time of writing. In short, he gives a concise background that will provide a good perspective for arriving at the total meaning, literal as well as the meaning for today. After this, the leader should read the passage aloud for the group.

A. Selecting the Passage

How long should the scriptural passage be? How much material should a group try to cover in each session? There is no hard and fast rule because the amount of text to be shared really depends on three variable factors: 1) the difficulty or complexity of the passage; 2) the perceptions of the group; 3) the depth into which the group wishes to go.

Some texts are really rather easy to read—narrative passages, for example—and much can be covered fruitfully in a short period of time. Other passages, by contrast, contain profound truths of great complexity that really need a great deal of exploration and consideration before their meaning comes forth (passages in *Romans*, for instance). If a group has developed great familiarity with Scripture and has considerable experience with sharing, it will be able to share more; on the other hand, if the group is still relatively new to biblical thought, the passage will have to be shortened in order to have time for the members to ponder words and phrases adequately. If the main purpose of the sharing is to introduce members to a whole book in a relatively few number of sessions, the group cannot dwell at any great length on a single passage, although it can always return to this passage again in the future.

Since the size of the passage will vary according to its difficulty and the competency of the group, there should be an overall plan of approach to the entire book. In that way, the group will not be bogged down in a few passages to the neglect of the whole. Because the group can always come back to difficult places at another time, it is generally better to keep plunging on.

B. Theme or Book?

Bible sharing is best conducted book by book instead of thematically or according to liturgical cycle of readings in the lectionary because the very structure of the Sacred Book is part of the revelation. God did not reveal Himself thematically or liturgically, but through the inspired hearts and minds of those who wrote and edited the books of the Bible. Each book, consequently, has a perspective—a theological outlook—which is itself part of the revelation. For example, the *Gospel of John* was constructed by its author with a definite theological understanding that comes out in the way the book is arranged; therefore, a Christian has a far more profound appreciation of the Holy Eucharist as a result of seeing it in the context of Jesus' dialogues with the Jews in John's gospel than he does by simply studying the sacrament in an encyclopedia article. While the study of doctrine is helpful, of course, it does not have the power of the word of God and is not the same as sharing the Bible.

C. Keep the Commentaries at Home

Furthermore, it is important that the discussion center on the text of the Bible itself and not on books about the Bible. Commentaries and guides are very helpful; the opinions of biblical scholars are to be sought and respected, but all that kind of research should be done before the group meets, and the commentaries should be left at home. If not, the group will begin to discuss the scholars and not the word. The sacred text itself must always be the center of attention.

D. Getting Started

We have already eliminated the Old Testament and *Genesis* as the starting point for Bible sharing. In the New Testament, the *Acts of the Apostles* is the best starting place, and after that read the *Gospel of Luke*, and then the *Letter to the Romans*. With these three books under its belt, the group will be able to determine for itself what books it wants and is ready to read.

We suggest *Acts* as the place to start because it is a rather easy book to read. It has good, strong narrative sections to hold the readers' interest and rich theological content in the sermons of the early Christian preachers to excite their faith. *Acts* also introduces the beginning Bible reader to the great characters of the New Testament: Peter, Paul, Timothy, Luke, and the others. At the same time, it gives us a world view of the early Christians which enables us to savor the gospels more because we see in the new, struggling Church the fruits of Jesus' victory over sin and death.

The Gospel of Luke, written by the author of *Acts*, connects us to the Jesus whom the Christian community of *Acts* was celebrating in their lives. Now, however, because of our experience with *Acts*, Jesus should have a newness and freshness for us that perhaps we have lost over the years through familiarity.

A reading of Paul's *Letter to the Romans* will cast the light of theological reflection on the meaning of the Jesus of *Luke* and the Community of *Acts*. Paul comes to grips with the basic questions of Christianity: What does it mean to be saved? What is faith? How do I live in the presence of God? What is the Spirit? Why the Jews?

At the same time, the group will be constantly reading the Old Testament, because these New Testament books make constant reference to passages in the Old Testament, and the time should be taken to read them in their original context. Although the Old Testament can be obscure to beginners because of the great distance in time and culture that separates us from them, it is impossible to appreciate the New Testament without the Old, and the best way of relating the two is to read the Old in the light of the New Testament references to it. After one has become imbued with the Scriptures, it will be profitable, as well as possible, to read the books of the Old Testament on their own and in their entirety, but it is not the place to begin. Also, a good Catholic Bible will have cross-references which will enable you to locate the related passages easily.

E. Private Preparation

As emphasized previously, group Bible sharing presupposes private Bible study as preparation for each session so that the participants will have something substantive to exchange with one another. There are many ways of studying individually, and there are many helpful study aids. Since the amount of time available, as well as your own motivation, will determine the extent you can delve into a particular passage, spend as much time in private preparation as possible so that you can read widely as well as in depth. Furthermore, take notes on the most important aspects of what you read, both to help you fix the points in your own mind, but perhaps even more importantly, as a means of sharing the fruits of your study with others. Although each will have a personal way of approaching private study, here are a few suggestions to help you get started:

1. Read the entire book of the Bible from which the passage you are going to share is taken so that you can get an overall idea of the book as a whole.

2. Fit the particular passage into the context of the whole book. How does it relate to the parts that come before and after it? This will enable you to grasp more fully the structure of the entire book which, as we said, is part of the revelation.

3. As an expansion of the above, you might also want to see how the passage relates to the entire Bible. Since the Bible is a unity in the Spirit, sometimes themes introduced by one author are only completed by a different author at a much later period (for example, Luke, completes Isaiah's prophecies concerning the coming of Christ into the world). Moreover, some teachings of Scriptures are the result of an evolution of theological understanding with the whole chosen people. For example, belief in the resurrection of the dead—the chosen

people did not always believe in it, as witness *Job*, but came to believe in it. (cf. 2 M 12:38-45) The battle was still going on in Jesus' day (cf. Mt 22:23; 1 Cor 15). Interrelating the books will help you appreciate the total tapestry of revelation. Again, the cross-references will help you.

4. Try to establish as accurately as you can the literal meaning of the passage. What does the author wish to reveal? Why did he write it? The introductions are particularly helpful for the general questions; commentaries on individual passages are also available and can be especially valuable in coming to understand confusing passages. In such cases, I particularly like *The Jerome Biblical Commentary,* which I think most people with a high school education can use, even though some may think it too technical.

5. Bible sharing does not stop with the literal meaning, so it is important that you try to find the meaning of the passage for today. What relevancy does the truth it contains have for the way men and women experience God in their lives today?

Another way of putting the same question is to ask: How have I experienced the truth revealed in this passage in my own life? For example, how have I experienced being chosen or saved (cf. Ep 1:3-14)? Trying to answer questions like this will reveal exciting things about yourself and how God is acting in your life right now.

6. Finally, all of this diligent but energizing study should be summed up in a few questions which you can make up to use as a discussion guide—even if you are not the leader! Although the questions you compose may not actually be used, still your forming of discussion questions that result from your personal study will make your contributions to the discussion stimulated by the leader's questions all the more substantial and helpful.

7. As a result of your careful study, you should have some good insights into the meaning of the passage to share with the group. You will also be more appreciative of the insights of others because you will be more capable of following the thought-process that has gone into forming the discussion questions and the attempts to answer them. You have a lifetime

to do it, and you will be able to grow each day in your understanding of the word of God.

8. Since all private Bible study, like the group sharing, is guided by the Holy Spirit, it should be liberally salted with prayer for divine wisdom.

9. After the discussion, you may want to make notes of the insights you have been exchanging in order to investigate for yourself some of the problems that were raised; the group's discussion, therefore, becomes a stimulus for your further private learning experiences. In particular, be sure to get in the habit of adding recommended books to your own bibliography. In fact, your group may well want to compile its own mini-library with books easily available to the group, or it may want to make contributions to the parish library so that the entire parish can have the biblical resources readily available for use. We spend so much money on buildings and programs, yet sometimes we neglect the obvious—a well-stocked and well-used library.

The Discussion Questions

The purpose of Bible sharing is to exchange with other Christians, in an atmosphere of faith and fellowship, personally experienced insights into the meaning of the sacred text and its relevance for Christian life today. Private study leads us to profound insight and new comprehension which we want to share with our group while at the same time benefiting from their insights into the same passage through group discussion. While each group will find its own rhythm of sharing based on the personalities and experiences of the group itself, an effective and flexible method of stimulating discussion and the sharing of insights on particular passages is through the use of discussion questions.

These questions flow out of private study and evoke rather extensive discussion as they are answered. While making up good discussion questions is admittedly challenging, experience makes it easier and the results make it rewarding; it gives us a chance to think creatively about the powerful word of God. Do not think each sharing session has to attempt to cover all the questions that have been proposed for discussion; answering just one question might occupy the whole period. In fact, prepare more questions than you can answer—it will make you want to come back to the passage again at a later time.

The following questions are just examples to show you some of the possibilities and to stimulate you to make up your own. These have actually been used to initiate discussion and have proven to be provocative of faith-building exchanges. The Scripture passage for which these questions were formulated is given in the parenthesis to the right of the title. The title, by the way, is a helpful device to use in summing up the basic points derived from the passage. Titles, of course, will vary considerably depending upon the reader and his perceptions of the passage.

I. *"The Divine Plan"* (Ep.1:3-14)

What does this passage mean to you personally?

How have you experienced its truths in your own life?

What is the "freedom" that the passage speaks about? Do you experience that? How? Do you experience a sense of release or of guilt?

What does it mean to be "chosen"? Do you experience that? How?

How have you experienced "the pledge of the Spirit"? Do you think that is too much to demand of religion?

What other Scripture passages could shed light on the significance of this passage?

Does the discussion of this passage make you feel uneasy?

II. *"Gospel Happiness"* (Mt 5:1-19)

What is the relationship of this teaching of Jesus to

the law of sin that Paul speaks of in *Romans* 7:14-24?
Do you think these "happinesses" or "blessings" can be experienced on earth? (Discuss each individually)
In what way have you experienced being the light of the world?
How does Jesus "fulfill the Law?"
Is this teaching of Jesus practical for life today?
Can you understand how living in the spirit of the beatitudes might bring down the wrath of others and lead to persecution for the Kingdom?

III. *"The Power of Jesus in Faith"* (Jn II)
What struck you most about the story?
Discuss the attitudes of Jesus, Martha, the Jews. What are they thinking? Feeling?
Why was Jesus so deeply moved (troubled)? Why did he weep?
What does this incident mean for you today?

IV. *"The Death of Jesus"* (Mk 14:42-15:47)
What is your general reaction to the whole incident?
Why is Peter's denial given such prominence?
Why did Jesus not reply to Pilate?
What do you think of Pilate's action?
Do you think Jesus despaired when he said, "Why have you deserted me?"
Wouldn't it have been better if Jesus had come down from the cross?
Why did the centurion say, "This was the Son of God?"
Why did Joseph of Arimathea have to bury Jesus?
How does this story strengthen your faith today?

V. *"The Resurrection"* (Lk 24:13-35)
How does this story compare with John 11?
What do you think of the story?
Why couldn't Jesus be recognized?
Why did he apprear to such ordinary people?
What is the connection between the Scriptures and seeing Jesus? What does that mean for us today?
What is the significance of the phrase—"Their eyes were opened?"
Why do you think Jesus vanished as soon as they recognized him?

VI. *"The Life of the Spirit"* (Rm 8:1-39)
What does it mean to be "spiritual" as opposed to "unspiritual?"
How do you know you belong to Christ?
Have you experienced the witness of the Spirit? How?
What is the relationship between suffering and glory? Consult other places in the New Testament.
What is the relationship between trials, triumph and God's power (Cf. 2 Cor 12:7-10)?
How have you experienced God's turning all to the good?

VII. *"Love in the Church"* (Rm 12:1-13:14)
What is the "new mind?" How do you put it on?
Does this whole passage sound practical for today?
What is your reaction to Paul's idea of civil authority?
What does this passage tell you about your gifts?
What are the other passages that refer to Christians as children of the light?
How would our communities be improved if we followed Paul's exhortation?

VIII. *"Faith and Love"* (I Jn—This would require more than one session to share adequately)

Why did John write this letter?
Do you think it is important?
What does it mean: To live in darkness? To live in light?
Do you find you are closer to those you love when you are in the light?
How do Christians (you) deceive themselves about sin?
Do you think this letter connects self-deception with fear? How?
What is the most important teaching of this letter?
How do the two commandments relate to the ten commandments?
What is the value of faith?
How have you experienced this?

Conducting the Discussion

The majority of the time in the sharing session should be devoted to actually exchanging ideas on the Scripture passage, and the key person in facilitating this discussion is the leader. Although some, of course, are more adept at leading than others, still it is important for Christian fellowship that the function rotate among all the members as much as is feasible. Experience is a great teacher, and with practice and ample opportunity, all members of the group should be able to lead adequately, if not well.

There are many books on discussion process and group leadership, and a group may want to purchase one for more detailed guidance. In the meantime, here are a few ideas about what the leader can do to initiate the discussion and keep it moving, always appreciating that the key to the successful meeting is the satisfying feeling that through the discussion all have grown in the word of God and the mystery of Christ.

1. The leader initiates the discussion by presenting the most suitable question he has composed. He may wish to

explain its significance briefly.

2. Through the formulation of his questions, the leader should have an approximate idea of the direction in which the discussion should go for the most fruitful exploration of the passage.

3. He should keep the discussion on target. However, if it takes an unexpected direction which is still fruitful, it should be allowed to continue, for if the discussion is too directed or constrained, it will falter and fail.

4. Once he has proposed his original question, the leader needs the courage to remain silent:

> A. Allow the participants time to think and speak; do not rush into talking, or feel that silence is unproductive.
>
> B. Do not allow the discussion to become a dialogue between leader and individual participants, or let the leader become the teacher.
>
> C. The leader should avoid merely commenting on everyone's contribution; rather, he should guide the discussion so that it builds on the good insights of each.

5. The leader should not so much participate in the discussion as encourage others to participate. Sometimes those who are more reticent need to be drawn out, perhaps through direct solicitation by the leader.

6. Be sure everyone has a chance to participate, but they should not be allowed to interrupt one another except in the usual course of conversation. Be sure that Christian respect is always observed.

7. Do not allow one person to dominate.

8. If someone is having difficulty making a point, the leader should try to help him clarify it, without, however, taking over the initiative.

9. If a serious dispute develops, it is best to pause for prayer with the leader expressing the need for divine guidance in the difficulty.

10. If the discussion gets bogged down in a question of fact

which no one can answer accurately at the time, the leader should encourage the group to postpone further discussion of it until the truth of the matter can be ascertained. It is then the leader's responsibility to research the matter and report back to the group.

11. When the question is sufficiently explored, or it is clear that the discussion is going nowhere, the leader should propose another question.

12. The leader should provide summaries of the discussion from time to time. At the halfway point is a good time to sum up where the group has been in order to help them ascertain the directions they want to go in the time remaining.

13. Another good place for summary is at the close just before the final prayer; it should be a general view over the entire course of discussion. Again, it should be brief.

14. The ultimate result of the discussion should be that the passage being considered is better understood at the end than it was at the beginning.

15. Just as the leader should start the meeting on time, he is responsible for seeing that it ends on time.

The Closing Prayer

The prayer at the close should sum up the experience the group has had of the meaning of the passage being shared. The leader begins the prayer, but all things considered, it promotes unity if all the members have an opportunity to voice their own sentiments aloud as part of the prayer. Some caution may have to be exercised to prevent the prayer from becoming too long. Many groups have found song to be most appropriate as a form of prayer.

CHAPTER ELEVEN

RESOURCES FOR BIBLE SHARING

We are fortunate today to live when books, pamphlets, newsletters on the Bible, Bible study and Bible sharing are in an abundance, and many of the best references are available in inexpensive paperback editions. Every Bible sharing group should devote some time to keeping up-to-date on the latest materials that are being made available every month; spend a few hours browsing among the current offerings at your local bookstore to see what selections can be helpful to your group. Publishers will also be glad to send you catalogues of their releases.

Frequent visits to your parish library to consult its biblical reference works are also recommended, but the tragic fact is that many parishes do not even have a library. Helping your parish to start one could be a very valuable contribution to Christian community life, provided, of course, the faithful could be motivated to make sufficient use of it to justify its existence.

Ecumenical Community Bible Centers

Some Bible sharing groups in a given area might wish to join together in a common effort to establish, maintain, and operate a centrally located Bible library and reading room so that the wider community could avail itself of biblical resources. Ecumenical interest could thus be roused, since individual church libraries might be prohibitively expensive for smaller churches and parishes. In many cities and towns a comfortable place where Christians might gather to study, read and discuss the Bible would be most welcome. While the hours during which it would be open depend on the local needs, surely volunteers could be found to staff such a delightful and important spot for growing in the knowledge of the Lord during the evening hours at least, say 7-10 PM on weekdays.

Audio-Visuals

In addition to books and publications, films, slides and tapes on the Bible are also available in growing numbers. These audio-visual aids can be valuable supplements to Bible sharing sessions. After my pilgrimage to the Holy Land, I had new appreciation of the Gospel message; seeing the lands where Jesus lived and ministered gave me new insights into the reality of His incarnation and the magnificence of the divine condescension to become man, suffer and die for us. It was evident to me almost at once just how formative the geography and the climate were in shaping the Gospel message. After my trip, Jesus' images and references were much more vivid and had greater impact on my spiritual life.

For example, following the way of the cross through the dirty, crowded streets of Jerusalem, surrounded by indifferent, if not hostile crowds of onlookers, gave me a new realization of the suffering Jesus endured on his way to his death. It could not have been an emotionally fulfilling "spiritual" experience for Jesus, yet without it, we would still be in our sins. To retrace his last hours in Jerusalem, or to gaze upon the same Galilean scenes that he viewed, brought the Gospel's reality to me in a way I had not before experienced.

While few have the opportunity to make such a pilgrimage, films and slides can be of tremendous help in conveying to us the influence his times and places had on the teaching of Jesus. How much more impressive to us are the mighty deeds he did, when we can retrace the steps of the man born blind—from the temple area, down the steep city hillside to the pool of Siloam. If this cannot be done in person, at least it can be seen through a series of carefully selected slides of the city of Jerusalem.

The *New Media Bible,* produced by the Genesis Project, has put the Sacred Scriptures on film. While it is expensive, if enough groups were interested to insure its utilization, it would be worth having, since it is a colorful visualization of the Sacred Scriptures.

Atlases of the Bible lands enable us to pin-point the scenes of Jesus' deeds, the places of the great teachings of the Old and New Testament and to appreciate the extent of Paul's travels under primitive conditions.

Nevertheless, the best resource you have is still your own Bible. Do not be afraid to write in it because God's word is living, and you keep it alive by making your Bible a personal book. The next resource is yourself and your group. You will be amazed at the wisdom, the insights, and the questions you share with your brothers and sisters in Christ.

The following bibliography is a very limited one, but it gives a beginning look at some of the valuable resources available for Bible study and sharing.

BIBLIOGRAPHY

BIBLES

Common Bible, Ecumenical edition (New York: Collins, 1973).

Good News Bible, Today's English Version (New York: American Bible Society).

Jerusalem Bible (New York: Doubleday & Co., 1966).

New American Bible (New York: P.J. Kenedy & Sons, 1968).

Revised Standard Version (New York: American Bible Society).

BIBLE ATLASES

Filson, Floyd V. and Wright, G. Ernest, *The Westminster Historical Atlas to The Bible,* rev. ed. (Philadelphia: Westminster Press, 1975).

The Oxford Bible Atlas is an inexpensive compilation of maps.

Pfeiffer, Charles F., *Baker's Bible Atlas*, rev. ed. (Grand Rapids: Baker Book House, 1973).

BIBLICAL CONCORDANCES

Joy, Charles R., *Harper's Topical Concordance*, rev. ed. (New York: Harper and Row).

New World Dictionary Concordance to the New American

Bible (New York: Times Mirror World Publishing, 1970).

Young, Robert, *Analytical Concordance to the Bible* (Grand Rapids: William B. Erdmans Co., 1975).

BIBLE COMMENTARIES

Albright, W. F. and Freedman, D.N., *The Anchor Bible* (New York: Doubleday, 1965). A whole collection still not finished.

Black, Matthew and Rowley, H.H., eds. *Peake's Commentary on the Bible*, rev. ed. (London: Nelson and Sons, 1962).

Brown, Raymond E. et al., eds. *The Jerome Biblical Commentary*, (Englewood Cliffs, N.J. Prentice-Hall, 1968).

Buttrick, George A. et. al., eds. *The Interpreter's Bible: A Commentary in Twelve Volumes* (New York: Abingdon Press, 1952-59).

Old Testament Reading Guide and New Testament Reading Guide (Collegeville, MN: Liturgical Press, 1960).

BIBLE DICTIONARIES

Buttrick, George A., *Dictionary of the Bible* (New York: Abingdon Press, 1962) 4 vols.

Gehman, Henry L., *The New Westminster Dictionary of the Bible* (Philadelphia: Westminster Press, 1974).

Léon-Dufour, Xavier, *Dictionary of Biblical Theology* (New York: Seabury Press, 1975).

McFarlan, Donald M. *Who and What and Where in the Bible* (Atlanta: John Knox Press, 1974).

McKenzie, John L., *Dictionary of the Bible* (Milwaukee: Bruce Publishing Company, 1965).

GENERAL WORKS

Anderson, Bernard W., *Understanding the Old Testament* (Englewood Cliffs, N.J: Prentice-Hall, 1975); *The Unfolding Drama of the Bible* (New York: Association Press, 1971).

Beck, Madeline and Williamson, Lamar, *Mastering New Testament Facts* (Atlanta: John Knox Press, 1973).

Blair, Edward P., *Abingdon Bible Handbook* (New York: Abingdon Press, 1975).

Brox, Norbert, *Understanding the Message of Paul* (University of Notre Dame Press, 1968).

Burke, John, O.P., *Gospel Power* (New York: Alba House, 1978).

Ciuba, Edward J., *Who Do You Say That I Am?—An Adult Inquiry into the First Three Gospels* (New York: Alba House, 1974).

Fitzmyer, Joseph A., *Pauline Theology: A Brief Sketch* (Englewood Cliffs, NJ: Prentice-Hall, 1967).

Gross, Heinrich, *A Biblical Introduction to the Old Testament* (University of Notre Dame Press, 1968).

Harrington, Wilfred J., *Explaining the Gospels* (New York: Paulist Press, 1963); *Record of Fulfillment: The New Testament* (New York: Image Books); *Record of Promise: The Old Testament;* (New York: Image Books); *Record of Revelation: The Bible* (New York: Image Books, 1963).

Heim, Ralph D., *Reader's Companion to the Bible* (Philadelphia: Fortress Press, 1975).

Humitz, Robert A., *Man Meets God: A Guide to the Great Themes of Revelation in Scripture* (New York: Benziger, 1971).

Hunt, Ignatius., O.S.B., *Understanding the Bible* (New York: Sheed and Ward, 1962).

Jarvis, F. Washington, *Prophets, Poets, Priests and Kings: The Old Testament Story* (New York: Seabury Press, 1974).

Kee, H.C., Young F. W., Froelich, K., *Understanding the New Testament* (Englewood Cliffs, NJ: Prentice-Hall, 1973).

Kunz, Marilyn and Schell, Catherine, *Neighborhood Bible Studies* (Wheaton, IL: Tyndale House).

Laurin, Robert B., *The Layman's Introduction to the Old Testament* (Valley Forge: Judson Press, 1970).

Léon-Dufour, Xavier, *The Gospels and Jesus of History* (New York: Image Books, 1970).

Link, John R., *Help in Understanding the Bible: A Guide for the Laity* (Valley Forge: Judson Press, 1974).

Martin, George, *Reading Scripture as the Word of God* (Ann Arbor: Word of Life, 1975).

McKenzie, John L., *The Two Edge Sword: An Introduction to the Old Testament* (New York: Image Books, 1968); *Light on the Epistles* (Chicago: Thomas More Press, 1975); *The Power and the Wisdom* (New York: Image Books 1972).

Neuenzeit, Paul, *A Biblical Introduction to the New Testament* (University of Notre Dame Press, 1967).

Reese, James M., *Preaching God's Burning Word* (Collegeville: Liturgical Press, 1975).

Small Group Bible Study Series (Minneapolis: Augsbury Pub. House, 1975).

Vawter, Bruce, *The Four Gospels: An Introduction* (New York: Image Books, 1972).

Wolff, Hans Walter, *The Old Testament: A Guide to Its Writings* (Philadelphia: Fortress Press).

PERIODICALS

Bible Sharing Newsletter (Washington: Word of God Institute) 4 times per year to meet needs of Bible sharing groups; answers questions that arise out of sharing experiences, passes on suggestions for improving sessions, bibliography.

The Bible Today (Collegeville: Liturgical Press, 6 issues per year.

AUDIO VISUAL AIDS

A Survey of the Bible, Filmstrip, record and guide (Alba House, Canfield, OH).

Basic Bible Course, Cassettes and workbooks (Contemporary Catacombs, 55 East Washington Street, Chicago, IL 60602).

Bible and Worship: Old Testament, 12 cassettes, study guides by Dr. Ralph Elliott.

Bible and Worship: New Testament, 11 casettes, study guides, by Dr. Reginald Fuller.

Biblical Inspiration, cassettes and study guides, by Carroll Stuhlmueller, C.P. (Argus Communications, 7440 Natchez, Miles, IL 60648)

Enjoying the Old Testament, George Montague, S.M., (program has four cassettes).

Enjoying the New Testament, George Montague, S.M., (program has four cassettes).

Eternal Word: Studies in the Gospel of John, Dr. Frank Stagg, four cassettes and response manual.

Evangelization and the Scriptures, John Burke O.P., program has four cassettes plus copy of speaker's *Gospel Power* (Alba House, 1978). Available from SCRC Tape Ministry P.O. Box 45594, Los Angeles, California 90045.

National Congress on Evangelization: Major Addresses (Word of God Institute, 487 Michigan Avenue, N.E., Washington, D.C. 20017) Burke, John, O.P., *The Vision of the Evangelist* (40 minute cassette) MacNutt, Francis, O.P., *The Power We Proclaim* (1 hour cassette).

The New Media Bible, the Bible on film with study aids, (The Genesis Project, Inc., 1815 West Market Street, Akron, OH 44313).

Toward Understanding the New Testament, edited by Laurence Boadt, C.P.S., program has 11 cassettes and manual (Paulist Press).

CHAPTER TWELVE

WORD OF GOD DAYS

Around the country from the east coast to the Pacific, from Canada to Mexico, there is a tremendous hunger for God's Holy Word. In large cities and small towns, rich and poor, well-educated and poorly-educated Christians are banding together in small groups to read the Bible together and share their understanding of it with one another, and more would eagerly join them if they were invited. There is a ministry opening up to members of Bible sharing groups that will have a significant impact on the Church of the future: it is a ministry of inviting others to grow in the word of God. The most immediate way of inviting others to grow in the word of God is to invite them to join your Bible sharing group. Opening up the groups to outsiders is important not only for those who are being invited to enter but also for the group itself. Each group will increase its understanding and faith by bringing new members into it through the outreach of love.

Now there is another opportunity for spreading the Good News: the celebration of Word of God Days in every region of the country. The idea of a Word of God Day is really very simple, and a group of dedicated Christians should be able to sponsor one successfully, since the Lord will be blessing your efforts as he promised: "Give, and there will be gifts for you: a full measure, pressed down, shaken together, and running over, will be poured in your laps" (Lk 6:38).

Basically a Word of God Day is a gathering of Christians to celebrate the saving power of the word of God. It is organized around a central theme which is particularly appropriate to the times, the region and the people and consists of three elements: a keynote address, workshops on the Sacred Scriptures and a liturgical celebration. Not only do these events provide immediate nourishment for the spiritual lives of those participating in the Day, they will also create a deep desire to establish and strengthen continuing programs in the word, especially through Bible sharing. While not much can happen in terms of acquiring extensive new knowledge in a few brief hours, much enthusiasm for continued growth in the Lord can be aroused which will motivate believers to continue in their ministry of personal growth and evangelical outreach.

The Keynote Address

After selecting the theme of your Word of God Day, obtain the services of a preacher who is willing to preach on that theme and who is capable of setting a tone that leads to enthusiastic participation in the events of the day. Since the purpose of the Day is not just to conduct workshops and increase knowledge of the Bible, but also to arouse a desire for ongoing Bible sharing, the keynote preacher should be a scripturally oriented person who has an attractive message of God's love.

While it may be difficult for small groups to obtain the services of well-known preachers, by having a Word of God Day, they can secure some very powerful speakers who would be willing to speak rather inexpensively simply because preachers welcome the opportunity to spread God's word. Thus, a Word of God Day makes the best preachers personally available to those who live in the remotest regions and smallest towns.

As part of the keynote address ceremony, enthrone the Holy Bible in a place of honor for the whole day. We began the National Congress on Evangelization in Minneapolis with a beautiful liturgy of enthronement: it was a very simple liturgy, but it created, from the outset, a sense of being in the presence of the Lord through His word. The songs were easily sung by the large congregation, and dancers led the procession of the Bible. Although the liturgy was uncomplicated, it was marvelously effective because it celebrated the real faith experience of those participating. All of these liturgical activities served to prepare the people for the preaching of God's word in the keynote address.

Workshops on Scripture

No matter how many books we read on the Bible, there is nothing like being exposed, in person, to a knowledgeable and creative teacher. Unfortunately, the best teachers are not always available to small groups in remote areas, but a Word of God Day gives even remote areas a chance to import them, perhaps from some distance, to conduct workshops on the topics that are especially confusing, important, or not well treated in contemporary writing. Furthermore, the personality of the outstanding teacher adds a new dimension to biblical study and has an immeasurable but most fruitful effect on both the understanding and the faith of those that hear them; the memory of the speaker's impact lingers long after the event is concluded, and the changes that he inaugurates by preaching the Word of God result in lifelong commitment to growing in faith.

Most of the finest teachers are willing to serve different groups and will accept an invitation if their schedule allows it. Sponsors will be delightfully surprised at just how accessible the "great" people are, if invited far enough in advance—at least a year.

Usually effective teachers will be happy to work with the sponsors in planning a workshop that is especially tailored to meet local needs: feel free to call upon their experience in setting up the best procedures for conducting the workshop. Give them freedom to plan after you have explained your needs, and most will be able to give you an exciting experience because their own enthusiasm for the topic is so contagious.

In a single Word of God Day, it is good to have a choice of

workshops without so dividing a limited audience that the workshops are too small to generate real excitement. Remember spiritual excitement and enthusiasm for more provide the motivation to build continuing programs of Bible sharing. Consequently, it is a good idea to repeat the workshops—once in the morning and once in the afternoon. This cuts down on the number of workshop leaders needed, and at the same time, it gives a chance for the participants to attend more than one workshop.

The Liturgy

Whenever Roman Catholics think of liturgy, they think of the Holy Mass. While a Mass is most appropriate for a Word of God Day, the Church also has a rich tradition of non-Eucharistic liturgies. For a Word of God Day it might be better to have a liturgy which emphasizes the importance of God's revealed word in the Holy Bible instead of emphasizing the Eucharist. This is not to downplay the Eucharist in any way; it is just to say that since we have Eucharistic liturgies available to us every day and every week, you might want to make the Word of God Day very special by emphasizing the centrality of the Divine Scriptures in the Christian life.

A creative liturgy committee can design very beautiful non-Eucharistic Liturgies, utilizing very moving scriptural selections which speak powerfully to the human heart today.

Because non-Eucharistic liturgies are a freer form, they allow for greater variation in design, and they avoid the problem of intercommunion when the Word of God Day is celebrated ecumenically.

The appendix contains the Bible Enthronement Liturgy we celebrated at the National Congress on Evangelization in Minneapolis in 1977.

Sponsorship

It would, of course, be most appropriate if the diocese or dioceses of a region, or even a group of parishes were sponsors of the Word of God Day, but even if you cannot get an official organization of the Church to sponsor it, the Church, with a few exceptions, would provide its approbation and assist in publicizing the event, and your bishop's presence in the celebration is always to be welcomed.

However, if for some reason, you cannot obtain official Church sponsorship, Bible sharing groups in your area can still band together to organize, fund and participate in a Word of God Day. In fact, there are probably many people in your area who would welcome the opportunity to join with you in such an endeavor for the Lord. It does not have to be a big extravaganza worthy of mass media coverage; frequently, the best kind of celebration is small, initmate and overflowing with a tremendous sense of mutual sharing and love.

While we want as many people to hear the word of God as possible, we cannot program events solely on the basis of numbers, nor can we measure success by turnout. The real test is whether we have been faithful to the word and given people a well-organized opportunity to grow in it. The key to this kind of success is the quality of the preachers and teachers you obtain. Famous preachers are famous because they are good and people enjoy listening to them—therefore, go for the big names. You will be surprised how many will be willing to accept your invitation, and in most cases it will not cost you as much as you were afraid it would. One day I spoke to a small group of only thirty-five people; after I got there, they told me that the previous week this same small group had enjoyed the services of Archbishop Fulton J. Sheen! Preachers like to preach, and all they want is someone to hear them.

Your local clergy, who are familiar with the preachers in the Church, will be able to suggest good preachers for your needs. In addition, look to authors of religious books which you found personally helpful; although not all authors are effective preachers, at least they have good ideas. Charismatic groups are familiar with the best preachers in the United States today, and probably have their recorded lectures available to which you can listen in order to get an idea of their suitability for your situation. The directors of continuing education, religious education and heads of retreat houses in your diocese will also have names to recommend, and reading Catholic newspapers will tell you of preachers coming to your area. Once you obtain your speaker, the rest falls rather easily into place.

Christian fellowship is essential to creating an atmosphere where the word of God can be shared in the Spirit, so recruit plenty of volunteers to assist in both the planning and the execution of the Day, and fill them with a sense of the importance of making all the participants feel totally at home and comfortable.

Model Word of God Day

There are many ways to arrange the program; the following is just one possibility. It starts late enough and concludes early enough for people to travel some distance without being seriously inconvenienced. The events are planned in a way that should result in a feeling of accomplishment when liturgy is celebrated as the climax.

9:00-9:30 AM   *Registration*

It is amazing how many details have to be taken care of in registration. Have enough registrars to get the job done in the time allotted. If you run behind at the beginning of the day, the whole schedule will be off. Always start and stop everything on time.

9:30-10:30 AM   *Keynote Liturgy*

Keep the liturgy simple so that the focus of the events falls on the Living Scripture—the preacher.

10:45-12:15 PM   *Workshops*

Do not try to crowd too much into an hour-and-a-half. Be sure to have enough workshop assistants so that your speakers can focus on communicating and not on housekeeping. Allow ample time for questioning of the speakers.

12:15-1:00 PM   *Lunch*

Allow enough time to serve everyone, but in a short day lunch should be a fairly quick meal. If it is prepared, be sure to have enough servers to serve it quickly; brown-bagging, on the other hand, is growing in popularity.

1:00-2:30 PM   *Workshops*

The morning workshops are repeated so that participants can attend at least two. Repetition also cuts down on expenses and keeps the Day firmly focused on the theme.

2:45-4:00 PM   *Concluding Liturgy*

The Eucharist can be a joyous celebration at the end of the Day because of its character as a thanksgiving service. But a Bible service can also be effective here, as a summation of the centrality of the Word of God in our lives. Whatever you decide to have, plan all the elements with a view to leaving the people walking on air. They should be excited by the end of the Day and filled with enthusiasm for continued faith-filled work with the Word of God.

APPENDIX

LITURGY OF BIBLE ENTHRONEMENT FOR THE NATIONAL CONGRESS ON EVANGELIZATION

Liturgy Of Enthronement Explanation

This liturgy was designed to bridge the gap between strangeness and fellowship. The Congress participants arrived in a strange city and hotel, and met many strangers, a situation which could have resulted in a "convention" atmosphere. We aimed, therefore, to create for them an environment of faith, mutual fellowship, and prayer so that the Word of God could be preached and shared in the Holy Spirit.

The first part of the program was devoted to the usual and necessary welcoming speeches—the greetings of the sponsoring persons to those who had given up so much of themselves to come and bear witness to the power of the Word of God and their desire to spread it. We were very blessed by God in the quality of our first speakers, the bishops who magnificently set up immediately the kind of atmosphere we had hoped to achieve. Because we did not want to come on too "churchy" emphasizing the split between worship and life, the bishops did not sit on the platform nor did they wear vestments: they came up from the congregation, and they wore their usual street attire.

It was only after the people had settled in that we began the liturgy of enthronement, which was marked by simplicity and directness. We were fortunate that in seating over 1000 people in a rather small hall, an atmosphere of expectation and excitement was created. The music had been carefully chosen

and the use of dancers added visual emphasis to the importance
of the Scriptures, recalling David's dancing before the Ark of
the Covenant. This liturgy took place August 26, 1977, in the
Minneapolis Convention Hall.

Enthronement Liturgy

Setting

A raised platform is erected along the west wall in the
center. (See sketch. It is divided into two areas: 1) Musicians'
and Speakers' 2) The first area is 24" elevation; the second is
30" elevation. Platform heights may have to be adjusted for
sight lines. In the musicians' area are the piano and chairs and
leader's microphone.

The enthronement area should contain an attractive
throne to receive a large, ornate Bible which is carried in
procession. It will be surrounded by candles carried in by the
Readers. It has to be large enough to accomodate dance
movement by 6 dancers.

The speaker's area contains only the podium, decorated
with a banner and a single chair.

Access to the platform is by three sets of steps; SR, SL,
Center which serves both levels of the platform. There is a
special section in the audience reserved SL of the center steps
for seven persons.

A preparation room adjacent to the platform area and
accessible for an entrance procession from the rear should be
provided. A lavalier microphone will be required for Fr.
Burke.

Song Practice

At 7:30 p.m. a song leader and pianist enter to lead the
assembled persons in song practice for the liturgies. Interspers-
ed throughout the practice will be other songs which will

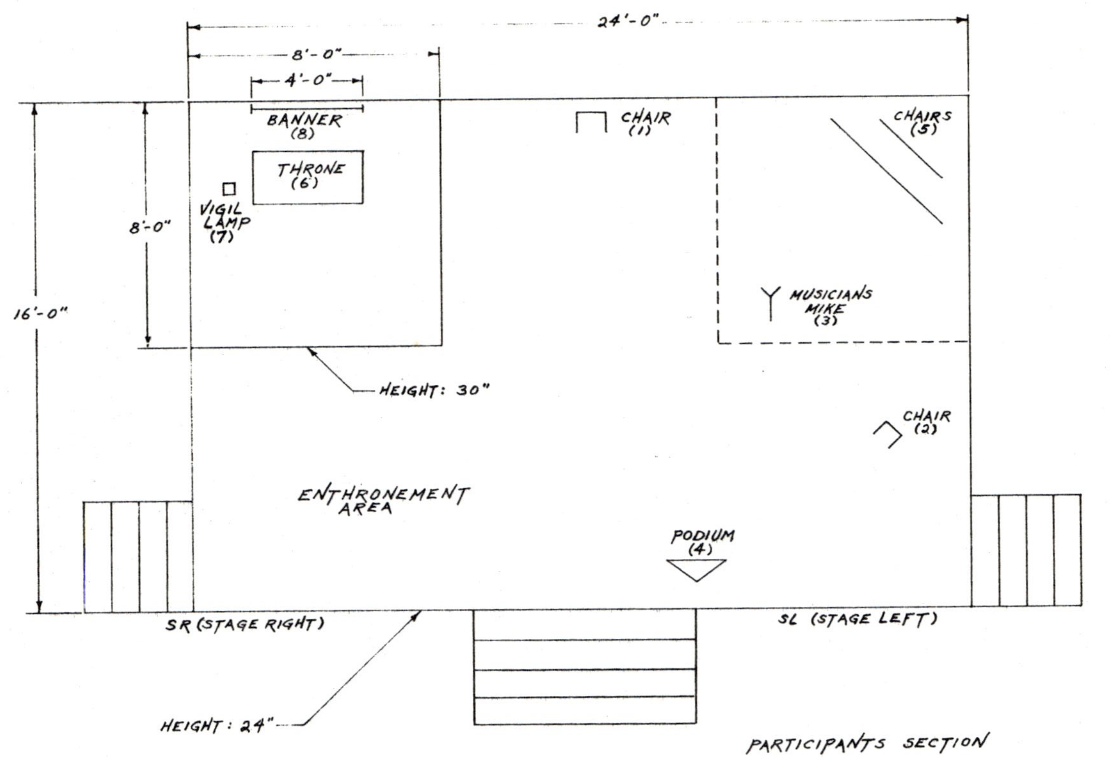

24'-0"
8'-0"
4'-0"
16'-0"
8'-0"
BANNER (8)
THRONE (6)
VIGIL LAMP (7)
CHAIR (1)
CHAIRS (5)
MUSICIANS MIKE (3)
HEIGHT: 30"
CHAIR (2)
ENTHRONEMENT AREA
PODIUM (4)
SR (STAGE RIGHT)
SL (STAGE LEFT)
HEIGHT: 24"
PARTICIPANTS SECTION

arouse enthusiasm for what is to come as well as to familiarize the people with the liturgical music. This 7:30 p.m. meeting will be announced in the program. At 7:50 the song leader will depart.

The Beginning

At 8:00 p.m. Archbishop Roach, Bishop Gallagher, both dressed in clerical black, should be seated in the reserved participants' section; they will be escorted by the master of ceremonies. With them are seated the four readers and the master of ceremonies.

The musicians enter and go to the music area; piano, two guitars, bass. They should be amplified.

The leader goes to the musician's microphone and invites participation in the antiphon:

> *Your Birth was not from any mortal seed but from the everlasting word of the living and eternal God.* (1 P 1:23, Music: Deeter Original)

The antiphon is sung twice. During the repetition the first reader comes to the speaker's podium. At the conclusion of the repetition he/she reads:

> *An Oracle of the Lord God.*
> *Do two men take the road together*
> *   if they have not planned to do so?*
> *Does the lion roar in the jungle*
> *   if no prey has been found?*
> *Does the young lion growl in his lair*
> *   if he has captured nothing?*
> *Does the bird fall to the ground*
> *   if no trap has been set?*
> *Does the snare spring up from the ground*
> *   if nothing has been caught?*

> *Does the trumpet sound in the city*
>   *without the populace becoming alarmed?*
> *Does misfortune come to a city*
>   *if the Lord God has not sent it?*
> *No more does the Lord God do anything without*
>   *revealing his plans to his servants the prophets.*
> *The lion roars: who can help feeling afraid?*
> *The Lord God speaks: who can refuse to prophesy?*
> *This is the Word of God.* (Amos 3:3-8)

After the reading, the antiphon is repeated.

> *Your birth was not from any mortal seed but from the*
> *everlasting word of the living and eternal God.*

The antiphon is sung by the song leader and people together. During the singing, the first reader leaves the platform by the SL steps and goes immediately to prepare for the procession and the second reader goes to the microphone. He/she reads:

> *The Word of God addressed to the prophet Ezekiel:*
> *"Son of Man, I have appointed you as sentry to the*
> *House of Israel. Whenever you hear a word from me,*
> *warn them in my name. If I say to a wicked man: you*
> *are to die, and you do not warn him; if you do not*
> *speak and warn him to renounce his evil ways and so*
> *live, then he shall die for his sin, but I will hold you*
> *responsible for his death. If, however, you do warn a*
> *wicked man and he does not renounce his wickedness*
> *and his evil ways, then he shall die for his sin, but you*
> *yourself will have saved your life. Thus speaks the*
> *Lord God.* (Ezk 3:17-19)

After the reading, the antiphon is repeated.

> *Your birth was not from any mortal seed but from the*
> *everlasting word of the living and eternal God.*

As before, the second reader leaves and the third reader goes to the podium. At the conclusion of the antiphon, he/she reads:

> *The Word of the Lord God was addressed to me saying, "Jeremiah, Before I formed you in the Womb I knew you; before you came to birth I consecrated you; I have appointed you as prophet to the nations." I said, "Ah Lord God; look, I do not know how to speak. I am a child!" But the Lord God replied, "Do not say, 'I am a child'. Go now to those to whom I send you and say whatever I command you. Do not be afraid of them, for I am with you to protect you—it is the Lord God who speaks!" Then the Lord God put out his hand and touched my mouth and said to me: "There! I am putting my words into your mouth. Look, today I am setting you over nations and over kingdoms, to tear up and to knock down, to destroy and to overthrow, to build and to plant. It is the Lord who speaks!" (Jr 1:4-10)*

After the reading, the antiphon is repeated.

> *Your birth was not from any mortal seed but from the everlasting word of the living and eternal God.*

As before, the third reader leaves and the fourth reader goes to the podium. At the conclusion of the antiphon, he/she reads:

> *At various times in the past and in various different ways, God spoke to our ancestors through the prophets; but in our own time, the last days, he has spoken to us through his Son, the Son that he has appointed to inherit everything and through whom he made everything there is. He is the radiant light of God's glory and the perfect copy of his nature, sustaining the universe by his powerful command; and now that he has destroyed the defilement of sin, he has*

gone to take his place in heaven at the right hand of divine Majesty.
This is the word of the Lord! (Heb 1:1-4)

After the reading, the antiphon is repeated.

Your birth was not from any mortal seed but from the everlasting word of the living and eternal God.

Convocation

During the singing of the last antiphon, Bishop Gallagher comes up from the participants' section by the center steps and goes immediately to the podium.

CONVOCATION ADDRESS OF BISHOP GALLAGHER

Welcome

Bishop Gallagher then goes to the chair which is SL of the podium and sits. Archbishop Roach comes up to the podium from the participants' section by the center steps, and welcomes the Congress to his archdiocese.

ARCHBISHOP ROACH'S REMARKS

Upon completing his welcoming remarks, the Archbishop leaves the platform and returns to the participants' section by the center steps.

Bishop Gallagher then rises and goes to the podium. He says:

God speaks to us. The Creator of all things reveals Himself so that we might live in His presence through love. His Holy word knows no limits. It is destined for all men and all women of every time and every place. It comes to us especially in the Sacred Scriptures. We so rejoice in this great gift that tonight we begin the National Congress on Evangelization by enthroning the Holy Bible in a place of honor where it will illumine our minds and enflame our hearts throughout the Congress.

Enthronement Procession

Having said this, Bishop Gallagher leaves the podium and platform by the SL steps, joining Archbishop Roach in the participants' section.

The procession enters from the rear.

The following order is observed: the thurifer; the four readers—two abreast carrying lighted candles; 6 dancers, women dressed in flowing robes; men dressed in shirt and pants; John Burke, O.P., in Dominican habit with cappa, carrying a large Bible, open.

The song leader cues the start of the procession by leading the congregation in the antiphonal song:

What You Hear In The Dark . . . (Earthen Vessels)

As they come down the aisle, the dancers dance joyfully but with restraint before the open Bible in accord with the song.

The procession comes up the center steps and the readers immediately place their candles at the four corners of the throne on the floor. They then move to stand up right and left of the throne. The dancers spread out in the enthronement area, all focused on the throne.

Fr. Burke then gives the open Bible to 2 of the dancers, who hold it while he incenses it.

The 2 dancers then slowly turn so the Bible is open US, and Mr. Graham moves US of the book, still held by the dancers. Meanwhile Fr. Burke moves SL of the throne.

Fr. Burke puts on the lavalier microphone at the chair and sits, saying:

Please be Seated.

Reading

As soon as all are seated, Mr. Graham reads:

> *With a large crowd gathering and people from every town finding their way to him, he used this parable: "A sower went out to sow his seed. As he sowed, some fell on the edge of the path and was trampled on; and the birds of the air ate it up. Some seed fell among thorns and the thorns grew with it and choked it. And some seed fell into rich soil and grew and produced its crop a hundredfold.* (Lk 8:4-8)

At the conclusion Mr. Graham leaves SR, and the dancers place the Bible on its throne. Fr. Burke steps to the front of the throne wearing the lavalier mike; the dancers turn toward him and he says, as if preaching:

> *Listen anyone who has ears to hear. The mysteries of the kingdom of God are revealed to you; for the rest there are only parables, so that they may see but not perceive, listen but not understand.*
>
> *This then, is what the parable means: the seed is the word of God. Those on the edge of the path are people who have heard it, and then the devil comes and carries away the word from their hearts in case they should believe and be saved. Those on the rock are people who, when they first hear it, welcome the word with joy. But these have no root; they believe for a while, and in time of trial they give up. As for the part that fell into thorns, this is people who have heard, but as they go on their way they are choked by the worries and riches and pleasures of life and do not reach maturity. As for the part in the rich soil, this is people with a noble and generous heart who have heard the word and take it to themselves and yield a harvest through their perseverance.*
>
> *This is the Gospel of the Lord!* (Lk 8:8b-15)

Dance

When he has finished, the song leader begins *The 16-fold Alleluia* and the dancers begin to dance by first coming together in front of the throne, as Fr. Burke moves to the chair in the speakers' section and stands slowly raising his arms in prayer.
The congregation stands and sings as the dancers dance:

16 Fold Alleluia

Sermon

At the conclusion of the song, the dancers complete their dance by sitting around the throne. When Fr. Burke goes to the podium, they all turn to him for focus.
The congregation sits.
Fr. Burke then preaches:

The Vision of the Evangelist

closing

At the completion of the sermon, the song leader goes to the music microphone and invites participation in the closing hymn.
During the hymn Fr. Burke, preceded by the dancers, leaves the platform, dancers SR steps, Fr. Burke SL steps.
This hymn concludes the convocation liturgy.

Rise Up O Lord Our God

At the conclusion of the hymn the leader of song invites all to go to the prayer vigils. He also makes any necessary announcements.